SUN RA
ART ON SATURN

SUN RA
ART ON SATURN
THE ALBUM COVER ART OF SUN RA'S SATURN LABEL

IRWIN CHUSID AND CHRIS REISMAN

IMAGE RESTORATIONS BY BARBARA ECONOMON

DESIGNED BY LAURA LINDGREN

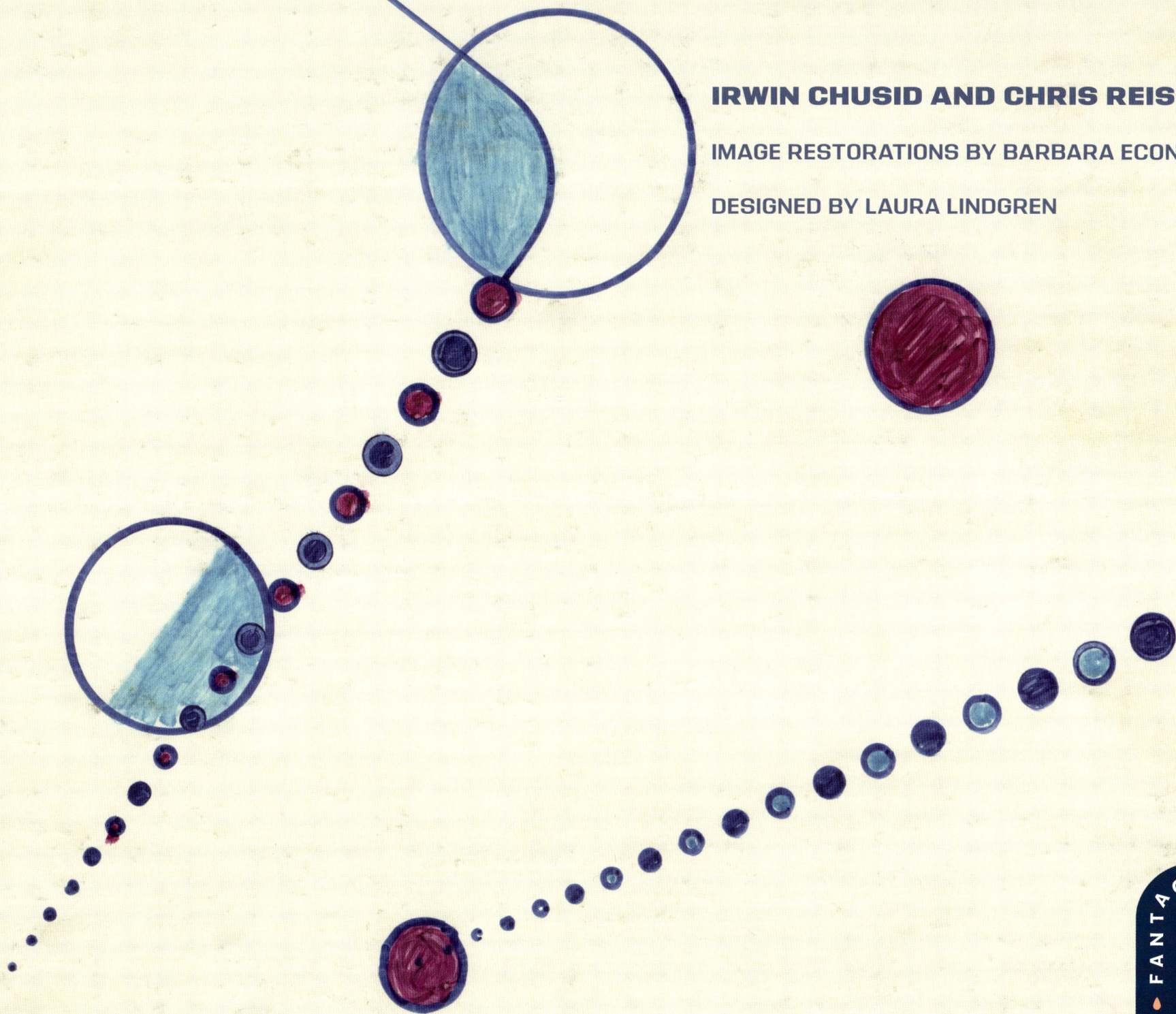

FANTAGRAPHICS

Editor: Irwin Chusid
Designer: Laura Lindgren
Associate Publisher: Eric Reynolds
Publisher: Gary Groth

Fantagraphics Books, Inc.
7563 Lake City Way NE
Seattle, WA 98115

www.fantagraphics.com
facebook.com/fantagraphics
@fantagraphics.com

PAGES 22-23: LeRoy Butler, detail from *Discipline 27-II* cover
PAGES 66-67: James McCoy, detail from *My Brother the Wind* cover
BACK ENDPAPER: Claude Dangerfield, detail from *We Travel the Spaceways* cover

ISBN: 978-1-68396-658-6
Library of Congress Control Number: 2022935192
First Fantagraphics Books edition: October 2022

Printed in China

CONTENTS

Introduction: *A Small Measure of Cosmic Justice*   **Irwin Chusid**

This is not a book about Sun Ra or his music. It's about packaging. Specifically, about packaging Sun Ra's music. More to the point, about the way Sun Ra packaged his own music.

Before streaming platforms, digital downloads, mp3s, cassettes, and CDs, there was 12" vinyl—the long-playing record. The LP is still with us, as are the "improved" formats that followed. But for several decades, the LP was not just dominant, it was virtually monopolistic (competing only with smaller iterations: the 7" single and the 10" EP). From around 1957 to 1988, Sun Ra (Herman Poole Blount, 1914–1993) self-released about 70 albums on his Saturn label in the 12" vinyl format. During the late 1950s and throughout the 1960s, most Saturn releases were sold in preprinted, standardized, artfully illustrated covers. Most of these are presented in this book's opening gallery.

In the 1970s, to generate merchandise more quickly—and usually in limited quantities—Saturn album design became a manual process. Labor was provided by the musicians who played in Ra's band—the legendary Arkestra—and by Ra himself. They lived as a musical tribe in a modest row house on Morton Street, in Philadelphia's Germantown district. This is where the handmade covers largely originated.

The pressing plant would ship boxes of black microgroove platters, each sheathed in a thin paper sleeve, and each required a protective cardboard outer sleeve. Stacks of generic, blank white covers were distributed to the bandmates, along with felt-tip markers, paint, glue, scissors, stickers, photos, and assorted bric-a-brac. Trimmed squares of transparent shower curtain were sometimes adhered as a laminate over hand-rendered designs. It was an ongoing arts and crafts project.

Saxophonist Marshall Allen has played with the Sun Ra Arkestra longer than Sun Ra did. (Allen joined in 1956; as of this writing in 2022, he's still leading the band at age 97.) Allen recalled the ad hoc factory:

The covers were done by the band. Everybody in the band made some. Sun Ra did a lot of them himself. We did 'em right here in the house. Once or twice, some of 'em might've been done by some kids who were around, but most of them were done by the band. It was a regular thing. Everybody would get ideas and design some covers, and we'd pile 'em up. I did some too. Paint, markers, glue—we had all that stuff in the house. We even had some old covers left from Chicago. We were always doing that.

The quantity and variety of handmade Sun Ra covers is vast—and unknowable. This book contains the best of what we've found. Doubtless there are other amazing specimens at large—spectacular artifacts that could easily replace a few

This photo of John Gilmore (photographer unknown), glossed with a trimmed patch of shower curtain, adorned a sleeve containing the Saturn album *On Jupiter*.

Sun Ra drawing for the 1966 Saturn LP *Other Planes of There* cover. The color motifs were never used, but the line art was adapted into a printing block for the commercial release (see p. 35).

Space Is the Place: The Lives and Times of Sun Ra, the artist explains: "I did never want to be successful. I want to be the only thing I could be without anybody stopping me in America—that is, to be a failure. So I feel pretty good about it. I'm a total failure. So now as I've been successful as a failure, I can be successful."

He was especially successful at selling flat, circular, engraved, petroleum-based by-products. The records acquired by Rounder sold out quickly. Many left the warehouse in the hands of Rounder employees, who coveted these treasures. Most were probably purchased unheard—they were instant collector's items. If Rounder received 200 copies of a particular pressing, there was a good chance they would never receive that album again. They couldn't order by title. They accepted whatever Ra shipped, and they never knew what was next in the pipeline.

Some wound up in the bins at Third Street Jazz & Rock, in Philadelphia. Proprietor Jerry Gordon recalled:

Some of the records he had recorded in 1956, '57, or '58, and they didn't come out until, say, 1965. Stuff from three different years and three different sessions would appear on a record. Almost always the records listed the wrong personnel. Some had no titles, no dates, no documentation. Everything to do with his label was confused, and I believe it was intentionally confused. He'd bring in a Saturn record, I'd sell out of it, but I could never get it back because he'd pressed a different album already. Some of them had no title, just a psychedelic design on the cover.

Artist Gilbert Hsiao, a longtime collector of Saturn LPs, loaned us dozens to reproduce in this book. These rarities are expensive, despite their often deplorable condition. "Many, many Saturns seemed to have been seriously abused while they were still in Arkestra hands," explained Hsiao. "I mean, they couldn't have been in worse shape if you were intentionally trying to beat them up. I'm not sure why that was, but I've heard this multiple times. My beat-up records were bought from a dealer who had come across dozens of Saturns, most in good shape but some shredded." It seems that with Sun Ra, artistic integrity is a given. Packaging integrity—not so much. (Audio mastering could be equally dodgy. In 1977 Ra issued on Saturn a live album known as *Taking a Chance on Chances*. All known copies of the LP have a defective pressing on Side A which renders it virtually

lesser-tier works included here—but book production eventually reaches a deadline. We're satisfied that what we included constitutes an excellent sampling of this idiosyncratic art form.

The records were sold at concerts, club dates, and via mail order. In the late 1970s, Ra landed a distribution deal with Rounder, thanks to Glenn Jones (whose personal chronicle appears later in this book). Jones would acquire from the band boxes of freshly minted LPs, each pocketed in a uniquely designed sleeve, often with little or no information other than an album title (maybe) or scribbling on the disc label. The paucity of facts about what was etched in the grooves implied an unspoken directive of sorts from Ra: don't worry about the details—just enjoy the music. Ra was renowned for mischief, mystery, and "misdirection." He was a polymath—musician, composer, bandleader, philosopher, poet, strategist, and sound inventor. He was the acknowledged pioneer of Afro-Futurism *avant la lettre*, and sheriff of the "Ra Jail." He was also a Cosmic Jester—and it wasn't simply a sideline. In John Szwed's essential biography,

Hand-colored sleeve, likely rendered by Ra himself, for the 1976 Saturn album *Live at Montreux*

Sincerely
John Gilmore

J. Wayne Dinni

Nimrod Hunt

Happy Spu. by
Danny Thompson
Bassoon + Alto

To You With
Love
All
EBAH

Space Age Greeting
from Sun Ra

Marshall
Allen
Oboe & Flute

Outer other BEIn-s/nE2iS
Tam Fiofori

Danny Dalvin
Alto + Flute

SUN ARTS

unlistenable. But it will still cost you a small fortune to buy a vintage copy even though you can't listen to half of it.)

There were certain recurring preprinted designs—whether tip-on art, pasted slicks, or stickers. But these multiples were not title-specific. Near-identical covers could contain *On Jupiter, Space Probe, Deep Purple*, or *Somewhere over the Rainbow*. With Sun Ra you got everything except consistency and predictability.

This book is a tribute to the covers—what they represent, why Ra did it this way, the uncredited artists and their artistry, the ridiculousness, the singularity, the DIY-ness.

Sun Ra's music was unconventional. His records didn't chart. Radio airplay was sparse, and he was never nominated for a Grammy. But in producing an expansive catalog of albums, each packaged in original works of art, Sun Ra gave his fans—and the music world—something they would never get from RCA Victor, Motown, or Columbia. Regardless of condition, Sun Ra's Saturn albums today sell for hundreds of dollars each. Used LPs on major labels are generally dumped at thrift shops or left at the curb.

For Sun Ra, it's a small measure of cosmic justice—a triumph of quality over quantity.

Irwin Chusid is the exclusive administrator for Sun Ra LLC, comprised of the lawful heirs and beneficiaries of the estate of Herman Poole Blount (Sun Ra). Chusid is the author of *Songs in the Key of Z: The Curious Universe of Outsider Music*, and co-author of four books about illustrator Jim Flora. He also administers the musical legacies of Raymond Scott, Esquivel, The Mighty Sparrow, Jean-Jacques Perrey, and Curt Boettcher.

Acknowledgments

MAJOR CONTRIBUTORS OF COVERS AND LABELS

Bill DeBauche	Mario Luesse
Will Ecke	Owen Maerks
Mats Gustafsson	Chris Reisman
Gilbert Hsiao	Lenny Silverberg
Glenn Jones	Tom Silverstein

ADDITIONAL CONTRIBUTIONS FROM

Eothen Alapatt	Peter Dennett
John Allen	Kieran Hebden
Jack Beard	Christopher Knott
Laura Brown	Craig Koon
John Colton	Alan Nahigian
Jeff Crompton	Mike Simonetti
Chris Cutler	Christopher Trent

THANKS TO

Michael D. Anderson/ Sun Ra Music Archive	Donald Kennison
Robert L. Campbell	Jay Millar
Cody DeFranco	Rachael Noel Fox
Jim Elferdink	Takashi Okada
Jerry Gordon	Kristen Pierce
Lisa Hirschfield	Lee Santa
Thomas Jenkins, Jr.	Quinton Scott
Leo Kaufmann	John Szwed

GREAT APPRECIATION TO THE FINE FOLKS AT FANTAGRAPHICS

Gary Groth	Jennifer Chan
Eric Reynolds	Lauren Peugh
Jacquelene Cohen	

A rare poster autographed by the Arkestra comprising two illustrations by James McCoy (1967), which were later featured on homemade Saturn LP covers (collection Lee Santa)

Saturn (and El Saturn) Discography   Compiled by Chris Reisman

Some years are approximate.

1957
Super-Sonic Jazz
recorded 1956, Chicago

1959
Jazz in Silhouette
recorded 1958, Chicago

1963
When Sun Comes Out
recorded 1962–63, New York

1965
Secrets of the Sun
recorded 1962, New York

Art Forms of Dimensions Tomorrow
recorded 1961–62, New York

Fate in a Pleasant Mood
recorded 1960, Chicago

1966
When Angels Speak of Love
recorded 1963, New York

Sun Ra Visits Planet Earth
recorded 1956–58, Chicago

Other Planes of There
recorded 1964, New York

The Magic City
recorded 1965, New York

1967
We Travel the Spaceways
recorded 1959–60, Chicago

Strange Strings
recorded 1966, New York

Interstellar Low Ways
recorded 1959–60, Chicago

Cosmic Tones for Mental Therapy
recorded 1963, New York

Angels and Demons at Play
recorded 1956 (side A) and 1960
   (side B), Chicago

1969
Atlantis
recorded 1967, New York

The Nubians of Plutonia
recorded 1958–59, Chicago

1970
Holiday for Soul Dance
recorded 1960, Chicago

Sound Sun Pleasure
recorded 1958, Chicago

The Night of the Purple Moon
recorded 1970, New York

My Brother the Wind
recorded 1969, New York

Continuation
recorded ca. 1962–63, New York

1971
My Brother the Wind Vol. 2
recorded ca. 1970, New York

1972
Universe in Blue
recorded ca. 1971–72, New York

Bad & Beautiful
recorded 1961, New York

*Sun Ra in Egypt: Dark Myth
   Equation Visitation*
alternates: *Nature's God*; *Live in
   Egypt Vol. 1*
recorded 1971, Cairo

Nidhamu
alternate: *Live in Egypt Vol. 2*
recorded 1971, Cairo

Horizon
alternate: *Live in Egypt Vol. 3*
recorded 1971, Cairo

1973
Dreams Come True
alternate: *Deep Purple*
recorded 1949; 1955–57 (side A),
   Chicago, and 1973 (side B),
   New York

Discipline 27-II
recorded 1972, Chicago

Monorails & Satellites
recorded ca. 1966, New York

1974
Outer Spaceways Inc.
recorded ca. 1966–68, New York

Space Probe
recording dates unknown,
   ca. 1962–72, New York (and
   possibly Philadelphia)

The Invisible Shield
recorded ca. 1961–63 and
   ca. 1967–68, New York

Out Beyond the Kingdom of
alternate: *Discipline 99*
recorded 1974, New York

Sub Underground
alternates: *Temple U*; *Cosmo-Earth
   Fantasy*; *Sub Underground #2*
recorded 1974, New York and
   Philadelphia

Monorails & Satellites Vol. II
recorded ca. 1966, New York

The Antique Blacks
recorded 1974, Philadelphia

1975
What's New?
recorded ca. 1962 and ca. 1975,
   New York (side A); unknown
   (side B)

Primitone
note: hybrid LP of tracks from
   Outer Spaceways Inc. and *Space
   Probe*, New York

1976
*Featuring Pharoah Sanders and
   Black Harold*
alternate: *With Pharoah Sanders*
recorded 1964, New York

Live at Montreux
recorded 1976, Montreux,
   Switzerland

1977
The Soul Vibrations of Man
recorded 1977, Chicago

Taking a Chance on Chances
recorded 1977, Chicago

*Some Blues But Not the Kind
   That's Blue*
alternate: *My Favorite Things*
recorded 1977, New York

Somewhere over the Rainbow
recorded 1977, Bloomington,
   Indiana

1978
Media Dreams
recorded 1978, Milan, Italy

Disco 3000
recorded 1978, Milan, Italy

Sound Mirror
recorded 1978, New York (side A)
   and Italy (side B)

Otherness
alternate: *Chromatic Shadows*
note: hybrid LP of tracks from
   My Brother the Wind Vol. 2 and
   Outer Spaceways Inc., New York

1979
God Is More Than Love Can Ever Be
alternates: *Blithe Spirit Dance*;
   Days of Happiness
recorded 1979, New York

Omniverse
recorded 1979, New York

Sleeping Beauty
alternate: *Door of the Cosmos*
recorded 1979, New York

On Jupiter
alternate: *Seductive Fantasy*
recorded 1979, New York

1980

I, Pharoah
recorded 1979–80, location
  unknown

Voice of the Eternal Tomorrow
alternate: *The Rose Hue Mansions
  of the Sun*
recorded 1980, New York

1981

Aurora Borealis
recorded 1980, location unknown

Beyond the Purple Star Zone
recorded 1980, Detroit

Dance of Innocent Passion
recorded 1980, New York

1982

Oblique Parallax
alternate: *Journey Stars Beyond*
recorded 1980, Detroit

1983

A Fireside Chat with Lucifer
recorded 1982, New York

Ra to the Rescue
recorded ca. 1982–83, New York
  and Paris

Just Friends
recorded 1982 (hybrid of new
  and old material), Chicago and
  New York

1984

Celestial Love
recorded 1982, New York

1985

Children of the Sun
  alternates: *When Spaceships
  Appear*; *Cosmo Party Blues*
recorded ca. 1982–84, New York
  and Paris

Cosmo Sun Connection
recorded 1984, location unknown
  (U.S.)

Stars That Shine Darkly Part 1
alternate: *Hiroshima*
recorded 1983, Montreux,
  Switzerland (side A) and 1985,
  Atlanta (side B)

Stars That Shine Darkly Part 2
alternate: *Outer Reach
  Intensity-Energy*
recorded 1983, Montreux,
  Switzerland (side A) and 1977,
  Bloomington, Indiana (side B)

1988

Hidden Fire Vols. 1 & 2
recorded 1988, New York

ADDENDA

Glenn Jones comments:

I contributed many entries to the first version of *The Earthly Recordings of Sun Ra* (including photos), many of which were carried over to the second edition, so it's possible some of the info in there came from me originally, including errors—if indeed there are any.

An overview of the distribution situation regarding titles:

When Rounder received albums from Ra with no title indicated on the cover or record label, I always called the Sun Ra house in Philly. (This happened no more than half a dozen times.)

In most cases someone picked up on the first ring or two. (I spoke with Danny Ray Thompson, John Gilmore, Marshall Allen, and possibly others.) I'd ask my question, and they'd shout, "Sonny, it's Glenn from Rounder. What's the title of that record we just sent up?"

I'd usually have to read back some of the track titles so they'd know which album I was referring to, and then I'd hear Sun Ra in the background give the title to whoever I was talking to, who relayed it to me. Once or twice Ra got on the phone himself to tell me.

There were one or two times when the band had left to go on tour, and I had to go with my best guess, based usually on whether there was a side-long piece that seemed a likely candidate for the title of the album itself. (Or maybe based on what the first song on the album was? I'm not sure I ever made a call based on that, but I might have.) At this point I can't remember which albums I took that liberty with.

Providing alternate titles in the discography may not clear up confusion, but at least it *limits* the confusion by giving the names of the possible alternate titles.

Chris Reisman is a longtime record collector and proprietor of Hudson Valley Vinyl in Beacon, New York. One of his specialties is Sun Ra album cover art. Irwin Chusid affirms that if not for Chris's involvement, this book would not exist.

Christopher Trent adds:

In general, the discography I did for the second edition of *Omniverse Sun Ra* (Art Yard, 2015) is more complete, accurate, and up-to-date than the *Earthly Recordings* discography.

Chusid tosses in:

A Tonal View of Times Tomorrow is a common Saturn cover, but there was no such titled release. It is a generic sleeve that was used for numerous releases starting in 1974.

EL SATURN

Presents

ON HI-FI
SLP 0216

JAZZ FROM TOMORROW'S WORLD

BY

SUN RA AND HIS ARKESTRA

VOL. I

An Afro-Space-Jazz Imaginary
The Printed Record of Sun Ra and El Saturn **John Corbett**

Sun Ra is now known globally as one of the architects of Afro-Futurism and the pianist and bandleader who, together with his extravagantly costumed ensemble the Arkestra, traveled the spaceways making interplanetary harmonies and melodies. But he began his life in 1914 with the quite terrestrial name Herman Poole Blount, in Birmingham, Alabama. By the time he was a teenager, Blount—nicknamed "Sonny"— was leading his own jazz band, and a dozen or so years of barnstorming and early recordings backing R&B singers eventually landed him in the Windy City in the mid-1940s. Chicago is where Blount became Ra, literally and figuratively. Along with his musical studies, Ra was a mystic and a self-styled prophet; he was widely read in philosophy, the occult, sociology, psychology, and spiritualism, and a die-hard fan of comic books.

He was befriended in the early 1950s by Alton Abraham, a young black radiology student with a keen interest in mysticism, outer space, the Bible, and science. Abraham would become Ra's manager and closest advisor for the following two decades. After Abraham convinced Blount to legally change his name—in the process transforming his identity—to Le Sony'r Ra (shortened to Sun Ra for public consumption), Ra formed and honed the earliest incarnations of his Arkestra, attracting musical accomplices including saxophonists John Gilmore, Pat Patrick, and Marshall Allen, who would remain loyal members of the band for most of their lives. (After Ra's death in 1993, Gilmore assumed responsibility for the Arkestra; Allen, 97 years old at this writing, has continued to lead the band since Gilmore's passing.)

In 1954, Ra and Abraham founded Saturn Records (alternatively billed as El Saturn, or Saturn Research), one of the first artist-owned labels. Working out of a base of operations in Chicago's South Side in the late 1950s and early 1960s, continuing at a distance when Ra relocated to New York in 1961, they created an array of objects as distinctive in appearance as they were in sound. With Saturn, Ra and Abraham issued LPs with covers that were designed and manufactured independently, some of which were handmade. By the 1970s, this was a normal state of affairs for Ra, who was by then based in Philadelphia and who, together with his bandmates, would decorate blank white records with hand-drawn designs. But earlier in his career, Ra's record design was oriented around printed multiples, deploying a small crew of grassroots, independent, semiprofessional black designers and local black-owned businesses in the creation of his label's unique image.

Among the many facets of his work, Ra's work as a producer can be understood as proto-postmodernist. He drew on a huge cache of tapes he had made starting in the 1940s, from which he assembled brilliantly hodgepodge records that willfully distorted his own historical development. On the space of one side of an LP he would place his more conservative—if often eccentric and highly personal—small group swing, big-band, and bebop tracks in immediate proximity with his more radical experiments in modal jazz, Afrocentrism, exotic polytonality, and aggressive improvisation. Though this kind of time-twisting, style-shifting variety revue was typical of Ra's later live performances, the pianist seems to have crafted the notion in the programming of his vinyl records. Just as he juxtaposed moments in his own musical development in the sound of the records, Ra assembled his LP jackets as pastiches of old-fashioned, even corny, jazz clichés mixed together with quite sophisticated 20th-century art ideas and nascent Afro-Futurist motifs.

Saturn's debut release was a 45-rpm single, conventionally packaged with a blank paper sleeve, but the record label had bold visual plans. In their respective notebooks, Ra and Abraham sketched out ideas for covers, mixing existing jazz and exotica tropes—cocktail glasses, dancing women, Kon-Tiki islands, Dali-esque surrealist landscapes, modernist abstract shapes, and the prevalent black and white pattern of the keyboard—with certain unique elements, such as spaceships, Egyptian imagery, and a kind of jazz apocalypse built of burning piano keys and tsunamis. Obsessed with crafting a special look, and obviously flush with optimism for Ra's artistic

Claude Dangerfield, preliminary sketch, *A Tonal View of Times Tomorrow*, ca. 1960

Claude Dangerfield, color separations , *A Tonal View of Times Tomorrow*, ca. 1960

future, Abraham allowed himself to fantasize about the design of a Saturn limousine and plans for a hi-rise Saturn head-quarters. Among several artists called upon to offer graphic designs for Saturn productions was a man named Claude Dangerfield. A friend and classmate of several of the Arkestra musicians at DuSable High, Dangerfield was an avid amateur artist. He was suggested to Abraham, who tapped him early on, in the mid-1950s, for cover ideas. According to drummer Robert Barry, Dangerfield also painted a mural in fluorescent colors on the ceiling of Gilmore's apartment.

The first designs Dangerfield submitted were wonderful, crude color pencil drawings that incorporated many of Abraham's and Ra's ideas. The most noteworthy thing about them was that, despite being ostensible plans for a record cover, they were horizontally formatted, not square, which was a problem Dangerfield rectified over the course of innumerable revisions. Indeed, the very first Saturn LP, *Super-Sonic Jazz* (1957), has what appears to be a Dangerfield cover (though he's

not credited). On the covers of many of the best-known early Saturn LPs and in many rejected designs from the same period, Dangerfield was required to cut and mix and hybridize his drawings, incorporating motifs from one into another, slowly morphing the images into something acceptable to both Abraham and Ra. In retrospect, this has had the same chronology-twisting effect as Ra's use of his earlier tapes in assembling the music for some of the LPs.

For one dramatic example, consider Dangerfield's design for *Sun Ra Visits Planet Earth*, which was originally conceived in the late 1950s, fully designed in the early '60s, finally issued with the record in 1966, and then cannibalized and very slightly redesigned for use as the cover to *A Tonal View of Times Tomorrow*, issued in various volumes starting in 1974. The idea of a cover gestating over a 15-year period—spanning the entire decade of the 1960s, including the psychedelic movement, which Ra helped inspire—is, in the mercurial world of popular music, unthinkable. But Sun Ra specialized in the unthinkable,

Snapshots of lost album cover illustrations, artists and dates unknown

Claude Dangerfield, color separations for *We Travel the Spaceways*, ca. late 1950s

in his musical pageantry, his philosophical pronouncements, and his record designs.

The most fully realized examples of Dangerfield's utopic-apocalyptic Ra covers include *Visits Planet Earth*, *We Travel the Spaceways*, and *Interstellar Low Ways*. For these, the artist hand-painted color separations on mylar (then a relatively new technology, invented in 1952) for each of up to eight colors; these were used to make offset lithographic plates, which were in turn printed in composite on paper. One Dangerfield cover, designed for *When Sun Comes Out Vol. 1*, was a beautiful disaster, with its red ink becoming virtually illegible when printed over a dark green background on bright yellow paper.

Owning the label allowed Abraham and Ra an unparalleled degree of control over their productions. The basic aesthetic of Dangerfield's covers is not too far from those of another musician-owned label of the time, Charles Mingus and Max Roach's Debut Records. Yet Saturn's production methods were unorthodox—piecemeal and self-taught—so where most labels used printing plants to produce their packages, in the

Unused composite lithograph with art by Claude Dangerfield for *When Sun Comes Out*

early period Saturn's LP covers were often made at home, in Abraham's makeshift basement printing facility. Although later versions of the first Saturn LP, *Super-Sonic Jazz*, were offset printed, Abraham claimed that the first run was silk-screened. No copies of this version survive, but a release from 1959, *Jazz in Silhouette*, was first issued with a two-color serigraphic cover attributed to one H.P. Corbissero. This may well have been a pseudonym for Ra, whose earth name shares its first two initials. Clumsily lettered, sporting a roughly drawn black stencil of an eye and bright red or fluorescent orange background, it has a coarse brilliance that is perfectly suited to the subtly détourned classic jazz it packaged. Abraham's ad hoc printing studio included several serigraph machines, though he used more conventional (and efficient) print techniques by the mid-1960s. In fact, in keeping with

Ra's penchant for scrambling his musical chronicle, many of the recordings of Arkestra music that Ra and Abraham recorded in the 1950s, releases that Ra fans think of as being Chicago records, would not see commercial release until after he moved to the East Coast in 1961. Abraham chose to remain in Chicago, and he administered Saturn's business at the time in partnership with Ra.

In this period, for the first time, Saturn began to use Sun Ra artwork on its new releases. In his cellar print lab, Abraham translated Ra's sketches, sent to him from New York, and readied them for press. Ra's drawings included careful design instructions, with reminders to print catalog numbers on the record cover spines for library reference (the archive being a consistent concern of Ra's). Ra executed his designs, which included swirling or spiky abstract automatic drawings, on

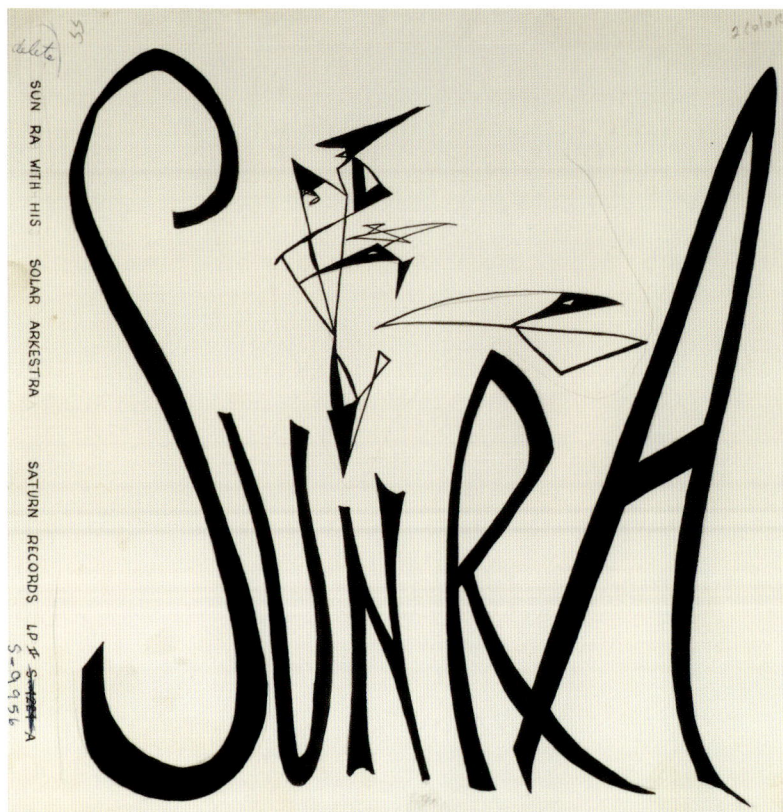

Finished cover (variant), *Art Forms of Dimensions Tomorrow*, illustration by Sun Ra, ca. early 1960s

tracing paper. Abraham had them redrawn in ink on board, from which a local die shop fabricated metal print plates.

On two mid-1960s records, *Other Planes of There* and *Art Forms of Dimensions Tomorrow*, Ra is identified as the graphic artist. In the initial production on both, the covers were directly printed onto paper (in the case of *Other Planes of There*, silver metallic paper), which was then manually wrapped around a blank cardboard sleeve, what is known as "tipping on." For *Art Forms*, two separate print blocks were used, Ra's name in blue ink and an abstraction in black ink. As separate, modular print blocks, they could be combined variously, the abstraction oriented in several ways relative to the lettering. These designs would eventually be offset printed (again, locally on Chicago's South Side) for greater quality control, but the originals, along with *Angels and Demons at Play*, also likely a Sun Ra design, were first printed and assembled by hand.

After a roughly six-year term in New York, circa 1961–67, Ra and the Arkestra permanently relocated to Philadelphia.

Abraham never left Chicago. Deploying an increasingly diverse pool of artists, some credited and some anonymous, Ra and Abraham continued to craft the Saturn image together throughout the 1960s and 1970s. On covers like *Discipline 27-II* (one of several designed by Ra's Germantown neighbor LeRoy Butler) and *Cosmic Tones for Mental Therapy*, a familiar strain of Afrocentrism entered the picture, while contemporaneous releases like *Sound Sun Pleasure!!!* and the stunning solo LP *Monorails & Satellites* continued to use Dangerfield motifs. Abraham turned to photolithography in certain cases, as on *Fate in a Pleasant Mood*, *When Angels Speak of Love* (which features an image of Ra that has been distorted either via Xerox or by fax machine, a new technology introduced in 1964), and the uproarious collaged image of Ra playing a lute on *Holiday for Soul Dance*. (The latter of these points out, even in its title, Ra's basic strategy of hybridization: tracks on the LP include "Holiday for Strings," "Body and Soul," and "Dorothy's Dance"—Holiday/Soul/Dance.)

Saturn commenced a parallel operation based in Philly in the early 1970s, directed by Ra and managed by saxophonist Danny Ray Thompson. These records are familiar to Ra collectors, often sporting 8½ × 11–inch Xeroxed sheets glued or taped to a blank cover—more guerrilla design approach than commercial (or even underground) print production. This move came as an answer to the band's mounting need for merch to sell at shows; the records were printed in small uneditioned quantities, often reprinted many times, making an already complicated discography additionally vertiginous. An impetus to hand-design, which may have started while the band was still in Chicago in the late 1950s, grew into a more extensive practice in the ensuing decades. Ra and his bandmates would decorate generic white sleeves with photographs, abstract line art, and ornate, multicolored Egyptian-themed drawings, heavy on metallic inks and felt-tip marking pens. Many extraordinary examples of these are showcased in the pages of this book, including some quite early ones probably from late in the New York period, a number of which are clearly in Ra's hand.

These cover designs sometimes utilized earlier offset "tip-on" record cover materials as starting points; they were drawn on, colored in, or cut down into excerpts and used as elements for collage. Others featured enigmatic linear hieroglyphic marks made with stencils, photos and drawings of Ra,

Print blocks, *Art Forms of Dimensions Tomorrow*

and endless mutations of Ra's name. The earliest of them are the most elaborate, sometimes filling the entire blank cover in patterns or text, often in vibratory hues, heavy on Ra's favorite color, purple. Such packages are Sun Ra reliquaries, decorated and then sold at concerts, unique twelve-inch artworks, precious gifts for the most devoted fans, housing the Arkestra's immortal remains—their music. Owning a handmade Saturn LP drew the listener into a one-to-one relationship with the musicians, sometimes Ra himself, exceeding mere autography, presenting a private artistic message for the record's new owner, colors and shapes and words specific not only to the particular production, but to that singular iteration.

As his reputation and ambition expanded, Ra seized opportunities to release recordings on other labels. The most extensive of these was a 1973 multi-record deal with ABC/Impulse!, which involved several new recordings and reissues of Saturn originals. The artwork on these, the most widely circulated of Ra's releases up to that point, was overseen by in-house graphic designers including Ruby Mazur, Alan Sekuler, and Tim Bryant. In the 1980s, the scope of Ra's non-Saturn releases continued to extend and included many other labels such as Improvising Artists, Philly Jazz, Hat Hut, Rounder, Soul Note, and A&M. Under these circumstances, the graphics were usually out of his control. But for a period of about two decades, with his own label Saturn Records, his accomplice Alton Abraham, designers like Claude Dangerfield and LeRoy Butler, and his merry band of DIY operatives, Ra had created an unprecedented and unique aesthetic, a blueprint for the look of Atro-Futurism.

John Corbett is a writer and curator based in Chicago. His books include *Vinyl Freak: Love Letters to a Dying Medium* (Duke University Press, 2017) and *Pick Up the Pieces: Excursions in Seventies Music* (University of Chicago Press, 2019). He is co-owner of Corbett vs. Dempsey art gallery and record label.

[A different version of this essay first appeared in *Art on Paper* (March/April 2009), and in *Microgroove: Forays into Other Music* (Duke University Press, 2015).]

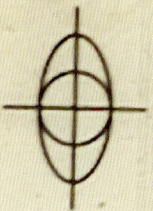

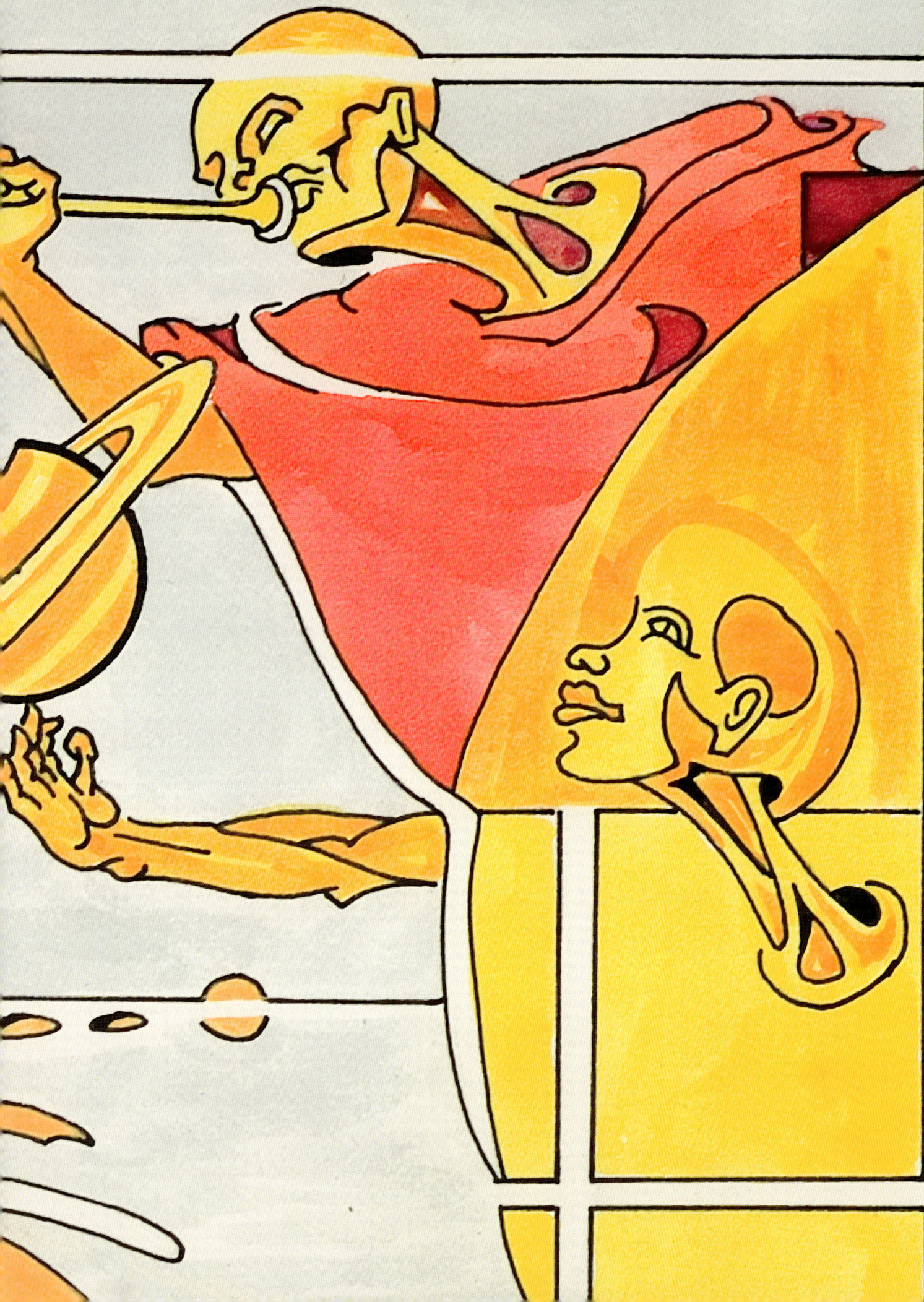

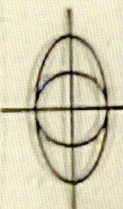

SUN RA and his ARKESTRA

1. Song #1
2. There Is Change In The Air
3. The Antique Blacks

(COMPOSITIONS AND ARRANGEMENTS ARE BY SUN RA)

℗ 1978
SATURN

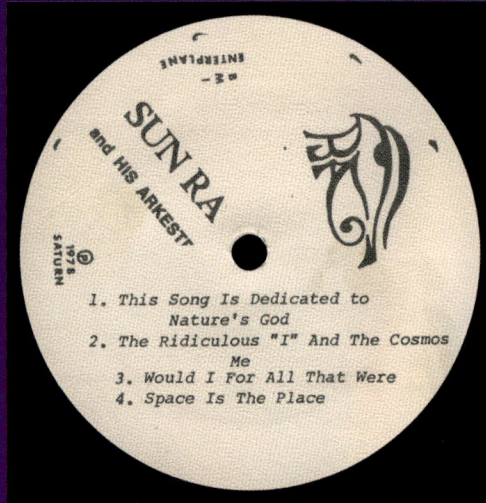

SUN RA
and his ARKESTR

1. This Song Is Dedicated to Nature's God
2. The Ridiculous "I" And The Cosmos Me
3. Would I For All That Were
4. Space Is The Place

℗ 1978
SATURN

SATURN
presents
SUN RA
and his
ARKESTRA
"DREAMS COME TRUE"

33⅓ RPM   SIDE A

1. DEEP PURPLE (S. Smith, Violin)
   (P. DeRose — Robbins Music Corp.)
2. PIANO INTERLUDE
   (Sun Ra, Enterplanetary Koncepts — BMI)
3. CAN THIS BE LOVE
   (K. Smith, P. James — Harms Inc. — ASCAP)
4. DREAMS COME TRUE (C. Williams, Vocal)
   (Sun Ra: J. MAYO)
5. DON'T BLAME ME (H. Randolph, Vocal)
   (D. Fields, J. McHugg, Robbins Music — ASCAP)
6. S' WONDERFUL (H. Randolph, Vocal)
   (I. Gershwin, G. Gershwin, Warner Bros. — ASCAP)
7. LOVER COME BACK TO ME (H. Randolph, Vocal)
   (S. Romberg, O. Hammerstein, Harms Inc. — ASCAP)

Saturn P.O. Box 7124 Chicago, Ill. 60607
485

1. When Spaceships Appear
2. Fragile Emotions Blues
3. Drummerlistics
4. Children of the Sun

5626 Morton Street Philadelphia, Pa. 19144

SUN RA

℗ 1981 Ra   enterplan bmi

33 1/3 RPM

1. AURORA BOREALIS
   (Ra)
2. OMNISCIENCE
   (Ra)

12480-A

P.O. BOX 7124 CHICAGO, ILLINOIS 60607

℗ 1981 Ra   12480-B
                   enterplane bmi

PRELUDE IN C# MINOR
(Rachmaninoff)

OMNISCIENCE
(Ra)

SUN RA AND HIS OUTER SPACE ARKESTRA

Celestial Love
(Ra)

Sometimes I'm Happy
(Caesar — Youman)

Blue Intensity
(Ra)

Interstellarism   EN TERDL BMI   ℗ C-1984-SG-3

AN INFINITY INC. PROD.   SATURN

5626 Morton Street, Philadelphia, Penn. 19144

SUN RA AND HIS OUTER SPACE ARKESTRA

D-1984SG-3   EN TERDL BMI

SOPHISTICATED LADY
(Ellington)

NAMELESS ONE # 2
(Ra)

NAMELESS ONE # 3
(Ra)

SMILE
(Chaplin)

SATURN   enterplan bmi

123180 B

IMMORTAL BEING
ROMANCE ON A SATELLITE
PLANETARY SEARCH
(Ra)

℗ 1981 Ra

EL SATURN

PRESENTS
SUN RA
AND HIS
A S T R O-INFINITY ARKESTRA
INTERGALACTIC SERIES II

SIDE A   ESR27363NP
                enterplan
                bmi
LONG
PLAY
33⅓RPM
520-A

BIOSPHERE BLUES
INTERGALACTIC RESEARCH
EARTH PRIMITIVE EARTH
NEW PLANET
(COMPOSITIONS AND ARRANGEMENTS
ARE BY SUN RA.)
520

P.O. BOX 7124 CHICAGO, ILLINOIS 60607

SATURN

SUN RA And His
ARKESTRA
Playing
"DANCE OF INNOCENT
PASSION"

33⅓ RPM   enterplan bmi

℗ 1981 Saturn

SIDE B   INTENSITY
                COSMO—ENERGY

Compositions & Arrangements are by Sun Ra

SATURN
5626 MORTON ST
PHILADELPHIA, PA 19144

SATURN

enterplan bmi

DANCE OF INNOCENT PASSION
OMNISONICISM

compositions by
Sun Ra
149℗

SUN RA AND HIS OUTER SPACE ARKESTRA

Celestial Love
(Ra)

Sometimes I'm Happy
(Caesar — Youman)

Blue Intensity
(Ra)

Interstellarism   EN TERDL BMI   ℗ C-1984-SG-3

AN INFINITY INC. PROD.   SATURN

5626 Morton Street, Philadelphia, Penn. 19144

SUN RA

D-1984SG-3

SOPHISTICATED LADY
(Ellington)

NAMELESS ONE # 2
(Ra)

NAMELESS ONE # 3
(Ra)

SMILE
(Chaplin)

EL SATURN

PRESENTS
S U N   R A   AND HIS
ASTRO INTERGALACTIC INFINITY ARKESTRA
DISCIPLINE   TWENTY   SEVEN

33⅓RPM

SIDE TWO
STEREO/QUAD   538-B
                     enterplan
                     bmi

"DISCIPLINE 27" 24:29
SPACE ETHNIC VOICE SUPPORT BY
JUNE TYSON, RUTH WRIGHT, SUN RA,
AND THE ENTIRE ARKESTRA

DISCIPLINE TWENTY SEVEN
PART ONE 9:05
PART TWO 6:59
PART THREE 5:00
PART FOUR 5:35

(Compositions and Arrangements
are by Sun Ra)

P.O. BOX 7124 CHICAGO, ILLINOIS 60607

SATURN
presents
SUN RA and his ARKESTRA

1217718-B   SIDE B
                   enterplan bmi

THIRD PLANET
SPACE IS THE PLACE
HORIZON
DISCIPLINE 8

Compositions and Arrangements
By Sun Ra

P.O. BOX 7124 CHICAGO · ILLINOIS 60607

SATVRN
GEMINI

THIRD PLANET
FRIENDLY GALAXY
DANCE OF THE COSMO-ALIENS

enterplan bmi

SUN RA

enterplan bmi

© 1985

1. When Spaceships Appear
2. Fragile Emotions Blues
3. Drummerlistics
4. Children of the Sun

5626 Morton Street Philadelphia, Pa. 19144

ENTERPLAN BMI

EL SATURN

© 1978 SATURN

enterplan bmi
CMLJ - A

DISCO 3000

(Ra)

SUN RA

P.O. BOX 7124 CHICAGO, ILLINOIS 60607

SUN RA & HIS OUTER SPACE ARKESTRA

ENTERPLAN BMI

B1984SG-9

A FIRESIDE CHAT WITH LUCIFER

AN INFINITY INC PROD — SATURN
5626 Morton Street, Philadelphia, Pa. 19144

Top Left (Album Cover)

SUN RA AND HIS ARKESTRA

SUPER-SONIC JAZZ

21st CENTURY EDITION

featuring JOHN GILMORE on TENOR SAX

JULIAN PRIESTER on TROMBONE

SATURN
LP 0216
HI FI

Top Right

SATURN PRESENTS

SUPER-SONIC SOUNDS

21st Century Limited Edition By

Le Sun Ra and His Arkestra

Magic Music of the SPHERES

POINTS ON THE SPACE AGE

This is the music of greater transition
To the invisible irresistible space age.
The music of the past will be just as tiny in the world of the future.
As earth itself is in the vast reach of outer space.
Outer space is big and real and compelling
And the music which represents it must be likewise.
The music of the future is already developed
But the minds of the people of earth must be prepared to accept it.
The isolated earth age is finished
And all the music which represents only the past
Is for museums of the past and not for
The moving panorama of the outer spacite program.

THE SPACE AGE CANNOT BE AVOIDED.

The prophets of the past belong to the past,
The space prophets of the greater future
Belong to the greater future.

The greater future is the age of the Space Prophet,
The scientific airy-minded second man:
The prince of the power of the air.
The air is music.
The air is power.
The power of the past was its music,
The greater power of the future greater
Greater music is art,
Is its greater music:
Art is the foundation of any living culture.
Living culture is skilled culture
Skilled dutifulness, aim and care
And love of beauty is the only way to produce art.

Skilled culture is the new weapon of nations,
The new measure of determination as to whether a nation
Is ready to be a greater nation is art.
A nation without art is a nation without a lifeline.
Art is the lifeline because art is the airy concept
Of greater living. It is the airy foundation of the airy
Kingdom of the future.
Tomorrow Beyond Tomorrow is the greater kingdom,
THE KINGDOM OF THE SPACE AGE. . . .

ABOUT THE COVER

With your mind's eye you are invited to see other scenes of the space age by focusing your eyes on the cover and your mind on the music. The scenes are from the space void.

THE COMPOSITIONS

These compositions are designed to convey the message of hope and happiness and a living measure from the better world of tomorrow. This is universal music . . . A free language of joy.

SIDE A

INDIA—A vibrant thought in sound, projecting to the mind the feel of the soul of India.
SUNOLOGY—A pleasant philosophy in sound. Sunology is a different kind of blues just like the sky is a different kind of blue. Sky blue is a daytime blue, the symbol of a sunny sky . . . CHARLES DAVIS, baritone soloist
ADVICE TO MEDICS—A leap forward into the better unknown; this is a SUN RA solo specialty.
SUPER BLONDE—Tells a happy story about a blonde who is just as super as someone else called super
SOFT TALK—This is a moving swingy concept of sweet nothings whispered in a manner modern. JULIAN PRIESTER is the trombone soloist.

SIDE B

KINGDOM OF NOT—This is not about a kingdom which is in the past, but it is about a kingdom called Not, which although it is not, yet is.
PORTRAIT OF THE LIVING SKY—A tone poem, a sound etching of rare beauty and life.
BLUES AT MIDNIGHT—Features JOHN GILMORE on tenor sax and ART HOYLE on trumpet.
EL IS A SOUND OF JOY—PAT PATRICK is the alto soloist.
SPRINGTIME IN CHICAGO—Features SUN RA on piano and electronic piano. JAMES SCALES is on alto.
MEDICINE FOR A NIGHTMARE—Features PAT PATRICK on baritone, JULIAN PRIESTER on trombone.

MAGIC MUSIC OF THE SPHERES

featuring

LE SUN RA, Piano
JULIAN PRIESTER, Trombone
CHARLES DAVIS, Baritone
JIM HERNDON, Tympani and Timbali
JOHN GILMORE, Tenor
VICTOR SPROLES, Bass
ROBERT BARRY, Drums
WILBURN GREEN, Electronic Bass
PAT PATRICK, Alto, Baritone
ARTHUR HOYLE, Trumpet
JAMES SCALES, Alto
WILLIAM COCHRAN, Drums

EL SATURN RECORDS · P.O. Box 7124, Chicago 7, Illinois

Bottom Left (Album Cover)

SR - LP 0216
ON HI FI

SATURN PRESENTS...

SUN RA and his Arkestra

Bottom Right

SATURN Presents

SUPER-SONIC JAZZ

21st Century Limited Edition by

Le SUN RA and his Arkestra

featuring

JOHN GILMORE, Tenor
JAMES SCALES, Alto
WILLIAM COCHRAN, Drums
JULIAN PRIESTER, Trombone
PAT PATRICK, Alto and Baritone
JIM HERNDON, Tympani and Timbali
VICTOR SPROLES, Bass
le SUN RA, Piano
CHARLES DAVIS, Baritone
ROBERT BARRY, Drums
ART HOYLE, Trumpet
WILBURN GREEN, Electronic Bass

All compositions on this LP are by SUN RA with the exception of SOFT TALK which is a JULIAN PRIESTER creation.

All compositions on this LP are designed to convey the message of happiness and hope, a living message from the world of tomorrow.

All compositions on this album are universal in scope. It has been said that music is a universal language. . . . THIS IS UNIVERSAL MUSIC, A FREE LANGUAGE OF JOY.

The Compositions:

SIDE A

INDIA is a vibrant thought in sound, projecting to the mind the feel of the soul of India.
SUNOLOGY is a pleasant philosophy in sound, it is actually a suite of which India is a part. Sunology is a different kind of blues just like the sky is a different kind of blue. Sky blue is a daytime blue, the symbol of a sunny sky. Charles Davis is on baritone. Charles is a real person, you can hear it in his playing. William Cochran is on drums.
ADVICE TO MEDICS is a leap forward into the better unknown. This is a Sun Ra solo specialty.
SUPER BLONDE is a happy story about a blonde who is just as super as someone else called super. Wilburn Green is on electronic bass; Pat Patrick on baritone; Robert Barry on drums.
SOFT TALK is a moving swingy concept of sweet nothings whispered in a manner modern. Julian Priester is on trombone; Patrick is on baritone.

SIDE B

KINGDOM OF NOT is not about a kingdom which is in the past but it is about a kingdom called Not which although it is not, yet is.
PORTRAIT OF THE LIVING SKY is a tone poem, a sound etching of rare beauty and life. Jim Herndon is on tympani and timball; William Cochran is on drums, and Victor Sproles is the bassist. Victor always plays with perfect intuition.
BLUES AT MIDNIGHT features John Gilmore on tenor; Art Hoyle is playing with a joyful sound, chorus after chorus of new ideas blending with the rhythm section which is moving like a touch of fire.
EL IS A SOUND OF JOY. Pat Patrick is on alto. Pat is a very creative musician artist.

SPRINGTIME IN CHICAGO features James Scales on alto. All you have to do is shut your eyes to look at Chicago in the springtime because Scales is painting the picture with his heart and soul. SUN RA is on piano and electronic bass with just the right touch. Scales is a most unusual altoist.
MEDICINE FOR A NIGHTMARE is full of fiery counter rhythms; the pace is terrific. Robert Barry is on drums; Pat Patrick on baritone; J. Herndon is playing tympani and timball; Green is on electronic bass; Julian Priester is on trombone.

le SUN-RA's arkestra is of CHICAGO origin. The group was organized four years ago, the musicians are CHICAGO musicians. Biographical material in detail will be issued with a later album. At present we will give you a bird's eye view of the past by stating that:

JOHN GILMORE formerly played with Earl Hines and Sonny Stitt. At one time, he was the leader of his own combo which played at the Bee Hive and Pershing Lounge here in Chicago.
PAT PATRICK has played with Buddy De Franco, Eddie Haywood, King Cole, Louis Belisco and Don Redman, Horace Henderson, Paul Bascomb and many others including Dinah Washington, Sammy Davis, Jr., Pearl Bailey and Larry Steele's smart affairs.
ART HOYLE with Lionel Hampton. . . . JULIAN PRIESTER with Lionel Hampton. . . . JAMES SCALES with Red Saunders of Club DeLisa fame. . . . JIM HERNDON with the Chicago Civic Orchestra, Red Saunders and others. VICTOR SPROLES with RED Rodney. . . . Ira Sullivan and Norman Simmons. . . . ROBERT BARRY, WILLIAM COCHRAN, CHARLES DAVIS and WILBURN GREEN are SUN RA proteges.
SUN RA has played with Stuff Smith, Coleman Hawkins and Luralene Hunter. Sun Ra was pianist for Fletcher Henderson and his orchestra during Fletcher's engagement at the Club DeLisa in Chicago. For the last seven years SUN RA has been co-arranger and producer of the Club DeLisa shows.

This is the first dimension of a new art-form. New because it is a blend of the East and West.

The art-forms of the past represent one particular country and one particular people, but since America is the melting pot of many countries and many peoples, the art-forms of the past are not suitable as basics for the development of the true American music.

America is a composite nation and only a composite music can represent the real America. THIS IS THE MUSIC.

The name RA is pronounced RAH.

COVER ART BY CLAUDE DANGERFIELD

RECORDING ENGINEER, WILL CONNOR.

SATURN RECORDS   4115 S. DREXEL   SATURN RECORDS

Jazz in Silhouette featuring John Gilmore. Images and forecasts of tomorrow.

WHEN SUN COMES OUT

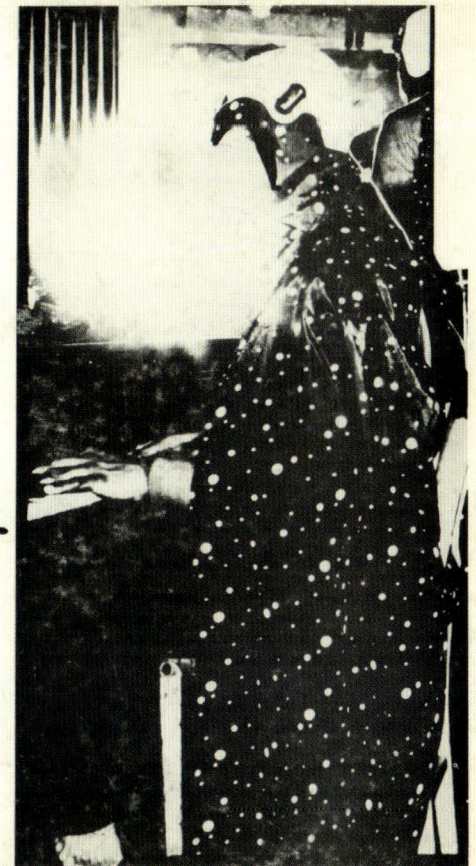

SUN RA AND HIS MYTH SCIENCE ARKESTRA

SATURN ® ©1965

SUN RA and his Solar Arkestra

THE POTENTIAL:
Beyond other thoughts and other worlds
are the things that seem not to be
And yet instinctively
How impossible is the impossible
Yet the impossible is a thought
And every thought is real
A thought that can bring to be
A seed that can bring to be
The reality of itself.
Beyond other thoughts and other worlds
Are the potentials . . .
That hidden circumstance
Cosmic control.

THE SHADOW OF THE FIRE
The vibrations of the sounds seem the same
But the meaning of the sounds
Take separate directions
At the crossroads
of the Cosmic-point of the arrow . . .
Beyond this Age
Through the darkness of the light years
And the light years of the darkness
Is the pure light of the pure darkness
And the pure darkness of the pure light.
The light is on the darkness
Became the light in the image
And the shadow of the fire.

FEATURING

JOHN GILMORE
MARSHALL ALLEN
PAT PATRICK
RONNIE BOYKINS
CLIFFORD JARVIS
ALI HASSAN
JIMHMI JOHNSON
CLIFFORD THORNTON
JOHN ORE
SCOBY STROMAN
MANNY SMITH

SIDE A
SIDE B

SATURN RECORDS
P.O. BOX 7124
CHICAGO 7, ILLINOIS
U.S.A.

Cosmic-Equations
POEMS
and
COVER DESIGN
by
SUN RA

MUSIC Composed and arranged by SUN RA
Published by Interplanetary (BMI)
Copyright © 1965

LP No. 9956
Stereo
Solar-Fidelity

SATURN 9954

SECRETS OF THE SUN

An album of compositions composed and arranged by SUN RA

This is the music heralding and reiterating the presence of another age . . . The Space Age. At this time since so many voices are speaking to the peoples of planet Earth, I hesitate to add my voice to the uproar, yet I find that what I have to say, I must say it now and since I feel that I can say things quicker by the medium and universal language of music, I have spoken.

More I need not say, except that we are moving rapidly and splendidly to a rendezvous with a better destiny; a better weigh and way of life.

SRA

SIDE 1

1. "FRIENDLY GALAXY" features SUN RA, piano; Pat Patrick and Marshall Allen, flutes; John Gilmore, bass clarinet; Calvin Newborn, guitar; Ronald Boykins, bass; Tommy Hunter, drums; Al Evans, flugel horn.

2. "SOLAR DIFFERENTIALS" features Ahrt Jnkens, space voice; C. Scoby Stroman, drums; Sun Ra, piano; Ronald Boykins, bass; John Gilmore, space bird sounds; Tommy Hunter, space bird sounds.

3. "SPACE AURA" features Pat Patrick, baritone; John Gilmore, tenor; Marshall Allen, alto; C. Scoby Stroman, drums; Eddie Gale, trumpet; Sun Ra, piano; Ronald Boykins, bass.

SIDE 2

1. "LOVE IN OUTER SPACE" features Sun Ra, piano; Marshall Allen, morrow; Jimmhi Johnson, percussion; John Gilmore, Pat Patrick, space drums; Ronald Boykins, bass.

2. "REFLECTS MOTION" features John Gilmore, tenor; Ronald Boykins, bass; Marshall Allen, flute; Sun Ra, piano; Stroman, drums.

3. "SOLAR SYMBOLS" features Sun Ra, gong and sun harp; Tommy Hunter, space drum percussion.

ALBUM COVER BY Chris Hall

SATURN RESEARCH 1973 P.O. BOX 7124   Chicago, Ill. 60607

S.P.A.C.E. MART

STROMAN
PATRICK
JNKENS
NEWBORN
GALE
SRA
M. ALLEN
EVANS
BOYKINS
HUNTER

J. GILMORE
J. JOHNSON

SECRETS OF THE SUN

SUN RA & HIS SOLAR ARKESTRA

CHRIS HALL

SATURN 9954

SATURN 9954

SECRETS OF THE SUN

An album of compositions composed and arranged by SUN RA

The compositions are:

SIDE 1   1. THE FRIENDLY GALAXY
          2. SOLAR DIFFERENTIALS
          3. SPACE AURA

SIDE 2   1. LOVE IN OUTER SPACE
          2. REFLECTS MOTION
          3. SOLAR SYMBOLS

SIDE 1

1. "FRIENDLY GALAXY" features SUN RA, piano; Pat Patrick and Marshall Allen, flutes; John Gilmore, bass clarinet; Calvin Newborn, guitar; Ronald Boykins, bass; Tommy Hunter, drums; Al Evans, flugel horn.

2. "SOLAR DIFFERENTIALS" features Ahrt Jnkens, space voice; C. Scoby Stroman, drums; Sun Ra, piano; Ronald Boykins, bass; John Gilmore, space bird sounds; Tommy Hunter, space bird sounds.

3. "SPACE AURA" features Pat Patrick, baritone; John Gilmore, tenor; Marshall Allen, alto; C. Scoby Stroman, drums; Eddie Gale, trumpet; Sun Ra, piano; Ronald Boykins, bass.

SIDE 2

1. "LOVE IN OUTER SPACE" features Sun Ra, piano; Marshall Allen, morrow; Jimhmi Johnson, percussion; John Gilmore, Pat Patrick, space drums; Ronald Boykins, bass.

2. "REFLECTS MOTION" features John Gilmore, tenor; Ronald Boykins, bass; Marshall Allen, flute; Sun Ra, piano; Stroman, drums.

3. "SOLAR SYMBOLS" features Sun Ra, gong and sun harp; Tommy Hunter, space drum percussion.

ALBUM COVER BY Chris Hall

SATURN RECORDS
U.S.A.

S.P.A.C.E. STROMAN, PATRICK, JNKENS, NEWBORN, GALE, J. GILMORE

SRA

M.A.R.T. ALLEN, EVANS, BOYKINS, HUNTER, J. JOHNSON

The Magic City   Sun Ra

SATURN — SUN RA & HIS SOLAR ARKESTRA — LPB — 711 — MONAURAL

SATURN — SUN RA & HIS SOLAR ARKESTRA — LPB — 711 — MONAURAL

SUN RA with his SOLAR ARKESTRA
"THE MAGIC CITY"

pat patrick..............baritone, flute   tympani on Cosmic "Eye"
john gilmore...............tenor
marshall allen..............alto, flute, oboe, piccolo
danny davis..............alto, flute
harry spencer............alto on side 1
robert cummings......bass clarinet
walter miller.........trumpet on side 1
ali hassan..........trombone on side 1
roger blank........percussion on side 1
ronnie boykins......bass
chris capers....trumpet on side 2
teddy nance......trombone on side 2
bernard pettaway...trombone on side 2
jimhmi johnson.....percussion on side 2

SUN RA ....clavioline and piano on "Magic City"
                    side 1
SUN RA ....bass marimba, piano, tympani, electronic
                celeste and Sun Harp, dragon drum
                    on side 2
Other drums by members of the Arkestra.

COVER ART BY WILLIAM WHITE
COMPOSITIONS AND ARRANGEMENTS BY SUN RA
PUBLISHED BY ENTERPLANETARY(BMI)
PRESENTED BY SATURN RECORDS

P.O. BOX 7124
CHICAGO, ILLINOIS
60607 U.S.A.

"FATE IN A PLEASANT MOOD"

SUN RA and his MYTH-SCIENCE ARKESTRA

"FATE IN A PLEASANT MOOD"

SUN RA

AND HIS MYTH SCIENCE ARKESTRA

SIDE A
THE OTHERS IN THEIR WORLD
(Ra)
SPACE MATES
(Ra)
LIGHTS ON A SATELLITE
(Ra)

SIDE B
DISTANT STARS
(Ra, Boykins)
KINGDOM OF THUNDER
(Ra, Allen)
FATE IN A PLEASANT MOOD
(Ra)
ANKHNATION
(Ra)

FEATURING:

john gilmore
TENOR SAX

marshall allen
ALTO SAX, FLUTE

ronnie boykins
BASS

phil cohran
TRUMPET

george hudson
TRUMPET

eddy skinner
DRUMS

sun ra
PIANO

SATURN RECORDS P.O. BOX 7124 CHICAGO, ILLINOIS 60607   LP SR9956-2-B

SUN RA and his OUTER SPACE ARKESTRA

NUCLEAR WAR
RETROSPECT
MAKEUP

compositions by Sun Ra

ENTERPLAN BMI

A1984SG-9

SATURN

℗ 1979 SATURN

72579A

33 1/3 RPM

enterplan
bmi

DAYS OF HAPPINESS
MAGIC CITY BLUE
TENDERNESS

(Compositions and Arrangements Are
By Sun Ra

SATURN

P.O. BOX 7124 CHICAGO, ILLINOIS 60607

1217718-A

SIDE A

enterplan
bmi

STARWATCHERS

DISCIPLINE 2

SHADOW WORLD

SATURN
P.O. BOX 7124 CHICAGO, ILLINOIS 60607

© 1978

SATURN
presents
SUN RA and his ARKESTRA

SATURN
presents
SUN RA and his ARKESTRA

EL SATURN

1217718-B

SIDE B

enterplan
bmi

THIRD PLANET
SPACE IS THE PLACE
HORIZON
DISCIPLINE 8

(Compositions and Arrangements
By Sun Ra

P.O. BOX 7124 CHICAGO, ILLINOIS 60607

© 1978

EL SATURN

SATURN
presents
SUN RA and his ARKESTRA
playing
OUT BEYOND THE KINGDOM OF

LONG PLAY
33⅓RPM

61674

SIDE B

enterplan
bmi

COSMOS SYNTHESIS

JOURNEY TO SATURN

℗
1974

(Compositions and Arrangements Are)
By Sun Ra

SATURN   P.O. BOX 7124   CHICAGO, ILLINOIS   60607

enterplan
bmi

SATVRN

SUN   SUN

I, PHARAOH
(RA)

℗
1979 SATURN

RA

RA

SATURN

enterplan
bmi
121771-A

℗ 1972 Ra

STARWATCHERS

DISCIPLINE 2

SHADOW WORLD

X1   Gil

RA

SATURN

enterplan
bmi
121771-B

℗ 1972 Ra

THIRD PLANET
SPACE IS THE PLACE
HORIZON
DISCIPLINE 8

SUN RA and his ARKESTRA

X2

"ANGELS And DEMONS AT PLAY"

Sun Ra AND HIS MYTH SCIENCE ARKESTRA

Presented by: SATURN "II" RESEARCH - Box 7124 - Chicago, Illinois 60607

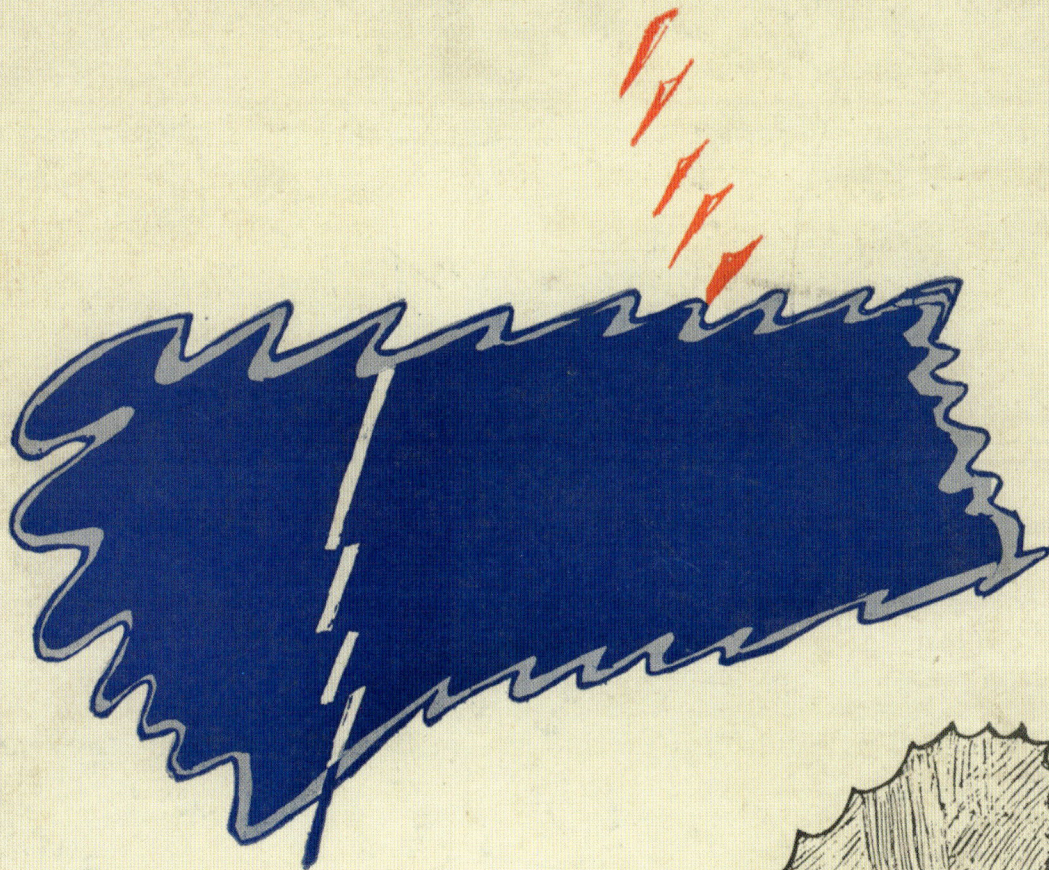

SATURN
Presents

Sun Ra
and his
Solar Arkestra

S-4226A

WHEN ANGELS SPEAK OF LOVE

SUN RA AND HIS MYTH SCIENCE ARKESTRA

sun ra
when angels speak of love
saturn lp 1966

WHEN ANGELS SPEAK OF LOVE

When Angels Speak of Love, they speak of higher minded beingness. Ecstatic sound vibrations interwoven by the mastery of SUN RA and his Arkestra into a Cosmic tapestry of warmth, beauty and illumination. Sound that calms the nervous system so that you can REALLY listen. Color that balances your aura° so that you are in harmonious attunation with yourself. An otherness of existence. A beingness so complete that where one really becomes a living, pulsating part of the Cosmo.

For When Angels Speak of Love they speak of the freedom gained from Cosmic Discipline. They speak of the freshness of not being possessed, as is the condition of earth-love.

When Angels Speak of Love, they speak of the accomplishment of evolving to a higher plane and reveling there with other Compatriots—the strength and beauty of an association with bimed beings who have an attunation of mind and spirit that is all encompassing as to render all earthly pursuits as dull and meaningless.

When Angels Speak of Love they speak of a dimension that is beyond the scope of ordinary earth-men. They speak of Tomorrow's World. And who should know better than Sun Ra, an Angel who has come back to show us!

Natel Juni

SUN RA
And his Myth Science Arkestra

SUN RA
JOHN GILMORE
PAT PATRICK
MARSHALL ALLEN
ALI HASSAN
WALTER MILLER
CLIFFORD JARVIS
RONNIE BOYKINS
ROBERT CUMMINGS
DANNY DAVIS

Piano
Tenor Sax
Baritone Sax
Alto Sax, Oboe
Trombone
Trumpet
Percussion
Bass Violin
Bass Clarinet
Alto Sax, Flute

celestial fantasy
the idea of it all .... side 1
ecstacy of being ....
when angels speak of love side 2
next stop mars ....

SATURN
1966 A
1966 B

SATURN RECORDS P. O. BOX 7124 CHICAGO, ILLINOIS 60607

SUN RA
"COSMIC TONES FOR MENTAL THERAPY"
and his myth science arkestra

SUN RA
and his
MYTH SCIENCE
ARKESTRA

"cosmic tones for mental therapy"

VOL. II 408
SOLAR FIDELITY
Stereo

SUN RA AND HIS MYTH SCIENCE ARKESTRA
"COSMIC TONES FOR MENTAL THERAPY"
VOL II 408

AND SUN RA SAYS:
"PROPER EVALUATION OF WORDS AND LETTERS IN THEIR PHONETIC AND ASSOCIATED SENSE, CAN BRING THE PEOPLE OF EARTH INTO THE CLEAR LIGHT OF PURE COSMIC WISDOM."

THE QUASAR (QUASI-STELLAR OR STAR—LIKE) EMITTED RADIO RAVES WHICH REACHED THE EDGE OF OUR GALAXY AFTER 13 BILLION LIGHT YEARS. AND SUN RA, WHOSE MIND-WAVES ARE SYNCRONIZED TO NATURE WITH COORDINATED INTUITION, PRIMED THE VOICE OF THE QUASAR ON A COSMIC TONE PIANO AND THIS THUNDER IS LIKE SHOCK WAVES SHAKING AWAY THE STAGNATION OF LIFE IN THE MIND. WHEN YOU CAN MOVE IN A DIMENSION FASTER THAN LIGHT YOU SOLVE THE RIDDLE OF TIME AND YOUR MIND'S COSMOSIS COMPLETES THE EQUATION: LIFE EQUALS DEATH, FOR IN THE EXPANDING UNIVERSE THE INFINITE DESTROYS THE ILLUSION OF LIMITATIONS WHICH TRAP MAN TO THE PLANET EARTH. THE INFINITY OF CONTINUOUS AND ACCELERATING MOTION CHASES THE FLEEING GALAXY ANDROMEDA WHICH IS 2 BILLION LIGHT YEARS AWAY FROM THE MILKY WAY AND TWICE AS LARGE. THE MUSIC OF THIS FLIGHT ENERGIZES THE QUASAR. AND SUN RA RECEIVES TONES FROM THAT QUASAR WHICH HAS BECOME PREGNANT WITH RADIATION AND THIS COMPLETES THE EQUATION: DEATH EQUALS LIFE IN A DYING UNIVERSE WHERE GALAXIES COLLIDE AND WHERE DEATH WEARS A MYSTERIOUS CROWN OF CONSTELLATION CALLED CREATION.

TO HEAR THIS MUSIC IS TO HEAR THE SOLAR BAND OF REVELATION. THE TONES REVERBERATING HERE PASS THROUGH THE TIME SPECTRUM OF THE ARKESTRA'S MIND AND YOU SEE WITH EAR AND WITH EYE AND YOU BECOME THE METAGENESIS OF COSMIC ATOMS, AND THIS ALTERNATION IS ALSO AN ALTERATION WHICH IS THE TRANSMOLECULARIZATION OF MAN'S FUTURE MIND. LIKE THE METAMORPHOSIS OF THE EARTH AS IT MOVES IN ITS 3 DIRECTIONS AT ONCE IN ITS THIRD POSITION FROM THE SUN, THIS MUSIC IS THE VOICE OF THE GALACTIC FATHER—CENTER. AND LIKE STAGES OF THE TRANSMOLECULARIZATION OF THE EARTH, IT CAN BE HEARD ONLY UNDER THE DRIVING POWER OF THE SUN.

THESE VIBRATIONS AND COSMIC RAYS ARE MAKING TONES FROM THE VOICE OF THAT FLEEING QUASAR AND THIS SUPRA-LIGHT REFLECTS THE ULTIMATE RHYTHM OF COSMIC MATHEMATICS.

AND SUN RA SAYS,
"THE COSMIC ROLES
ARE WRITTEN ON SUNDRY PARCHMENTS
TINTED WITH FIRE
BLUE VIBRATIONS OF PULSATING FLAME
ENERGIES. . . G—FORCE DIMENSIONS
ABSTRACT PLANES OF SONIC AND SIGHT."
—Hank Dunera

AND OTHERNESS, SUN RA, Cosmic Side Drums, Clavoline; MARSHALL ALLEN, Oboe; JOHN GILMORE, Bass Clarinet.

THITHER AND YON, MARSHALL ALLEN, Oboe; RONNIE BOYKINS, Bass. JOHN GILMORE, Sky Tone Drums; ROBERT CUMMINGS, Bass Clarinet; DANNY DAVIS, Flute; PAT PATRICK, Flute; CLIFFORD JARVIS, Drums; T. HUNTER, Percussion.

ADVENTURE EQUATION, SUN RA, Organ; JOHN GILMORE, Bass Clarinet, Sky Drums; MARSHALL ALLEN, Alto, Astro Space Drums; RONNIE BOYKINS, Bass.

MOON DANCE, RONNIE BOYKINS, Bass; SUN RA, Astro Space Organ; C. JARVIS, Percussion.

VOICE OF SPACE SUN RA, Astro Space Organ; RONNIE BOYKINS, Bass, DANNY DAVIS, Alto; JOHN GILMORE, Sky Drums,

FEATURING

SUN RA, Organ, Clavoline, Cosmic Side Drum
JOHN GILMORE, Bass Clarinet
PAT PATRICK, Baritone Sax
MARSHALL ALLEN, Oboe, Flute, Alto
RONNIE BOYKINS, Bass
DANNY DAVIS, Alto, Flute
ROBERT CUMMINGS, Baritone Clarinet
JAMES JACKSON, Log Drums, Flute
CLIFFORD JARVIS, Percussion
T. HUNTER, Percussion

SIDE A
AND OTHERNESS;
THITHER AND YON;
ADVENTURE-EQUATION;
SIDE B
MOON DANCE;
VOICE OF SPACE;

Compositions and arrangements are by SUN RA
Published by ENTERPLANETARY BMI ©

Cover Art: RICHARD PEDREGUERA
Recording Engineer: A. Abraham
Studio: EL SATURN
A Product of Inhfinity, Inc. Chicago, Illinois

RUMPELSTILSKIN
(RA)

IMAGES
(RA)

enterplan
bmi

℗ 1979 SATURN

S EL

SATURN
presents
SUN RA and his ARKESTRA
playing

LONG
PLAY

33⅓ RPM

I44000B

SIDE B.

enterplan
bmi

ISLAND IN THE SUN

THE INVISIBLE SHIELD

JANUS

℗ 1977

SATURN

(Compositions and Arrangements Are)
By Sun Ra

P.O. BOX 7124 CHICAGO, ILLINOIS 60607

THOTH

INTERGALACTIC

ENTERPLAN
BMI

SIDE 2
33 1/3 RPM
1272-B

PRESENTS
S U N   R A
AND HIS
ASTRO-INTERGALACTIC-INFINITY-ARKESTRA
PLAYING
"NATURE'S GOD"
FRIENDLY GALAXY No. 2
TO NATURES GOD
WHY GO TO THE MOON?
[COMPOSITIONS AND ARRANGEMENTS
ARE BY, SUN RA]

P.O. BOX 7124 CHICAGO, ILLINOIS 60607

Enterplanetary
Koncepts
BMI

SATURN XI

B
℗ 1983 SATURN

just friends (klenner-lewis)
under the spell of love (Ra)
dancing shadows (Ra)

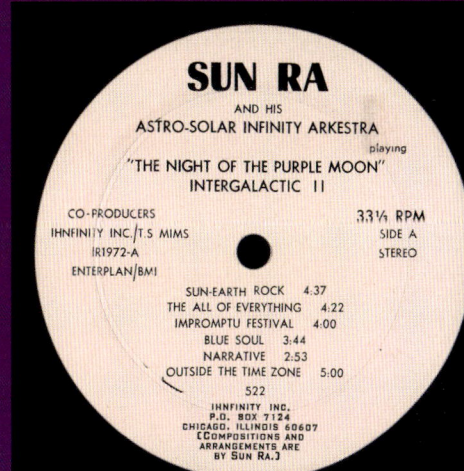

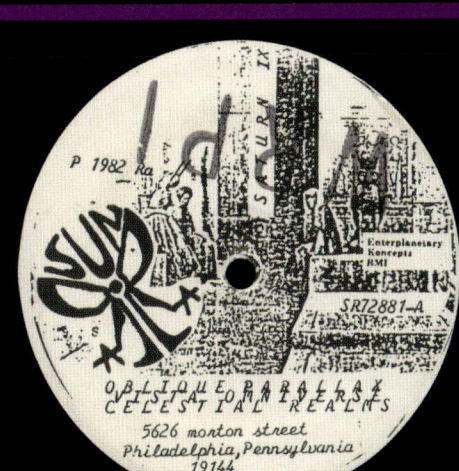

SUN-RA and his myth Science Arkestra PLAYS INTERSTELLAR LOW WAYS

SUN RA and his MYTH SCIENCE ARKESTRA

interstellar low ways

formerly

"ROCKET NUMBER NINE TAKE OFF FOR THE PLANET VENUS"

"THE IMPOSSIBLE IS THE WATCHWORD OF THE GREATER SPACE AGE" THE SPACE AGE CANNOT BE AVOIDED AND THE SPACE MUSIC IS THE KEY TO UNDERSTANDING THE MEANING OF THE IMPOSSIBLE AND EVERY OTHER ENIGMA. —SUN RA

FEATURING

SUN RA, Piano,
JOHN GILMORE, Tenor,
PAT PATRICK, Baritone, Flute
MARSHALL ALLEN, Flute, Alto
RONNIE BOYKINS, Bass
PHIL CORHAN, Trumpet
GEORGE HUDSON, Trumpet
EDWARD SKINNER, Percussion
WILLIAM COCHRAN, Percussion

Recording Engineer: A. Abraham
Studio: EL SATURN
A Product of Infinity, Inc. Chicago, Illinois

ONWARD George Hudson, Trumpet., John Gilmore, Tenor. Sun Ra, Piano.

SOMEWHERE IN SPACE Sun Ra, Piano, John Gilmore, Tenor, Marshall Allen, Flute., Ronnie Boykins Bas.

INTERPLANETARY MUSIC, Sun Ra, Piano, Vocal by the Arkestra; Ronnie Boykins, Bass, Space Gong. Interplay by Sun Ra.

INTERSTELLAR LOWAYS, Sun Ra, Piano; Theme Melody John Gilmore, Tenor; Marshall Allen and Pat Patrick, on flute; followed with Marshall Allen on Flute; Sun Ra, Piano; William Cochran on Drums; Ronnie Boykins, Bass; again Sun Ra, Piano, Chimes, Gong; Pat Patrick, Bells and Claves.

SPACE LONELINESS, Phil Corhan, Trumpet; Sun Ra, Piano; Marshall Allen, Alto.

SPACE AURA, Sun Ra, Piano; George Hudson, Trumpet; John Gilmore, Tenor; George Hudson, Trumpet.

ROCKET NUMBER NINE. Vocal by the Arkestra; Edward Skinner, Drums; Sun Ra, Piano; John Gilmore, Tenor; Ronnie Boykins, Bass; Sun Ra, Piano.

LP - 203

SUN RA AND HIS AND HIS MYTH SCIENCE ARKESTRA — "ROCKET NUMBER NINE TAKE OFF FOR PLANET VENUS"

SIDE A
ONWARD
SOMEWHERE IN SPACE
INTERPLANETARY MUSIC
INTERSTELLAR LOW WAYS

SIDE B
SPACE LONELINESS
SPACE AURA
ROCKET NUMBER NINE TAKE OFF
FOR PLANET VENUS

Compositions and arrangements by SUN RA
Published by ENTERPLANETARY BMI copyright

SOLAR FIDELITY LP - 203

EL SATURN RECORDS -   P.O. BOX 7124 -   CHICAGO, ILLINOIS

SUN-RA and his ASTRO INFINITY ARKESTRA "STRANGE STRINGS"

Cat. No. 502
Solar Fidelity

SUN RA and his ASTRO INFINITY "STRANGE STRINGS" ARKESTRA

STRANGE STRINGS

ELECTRONIC STRINGS
BY
SUN RA
JOHN GILMORE, PAT PATRICK,
MARSHALL ALLEN, DANNY DAVIS,
ALI HARSAN, ROBERT CUMMINS,
JAMES JACSON, THLAN ALDRIDGE
CARL NIMROD

SPACE VOICE
THLAN ALDRIDGE

TYMPANI
CLIFFORD JARVIS
SUN RA

PERCUSSION
CLIFFORD JARVIS

ELECTRONIC PIANO – LIGHTNING DRUM
SUN RA

OBOE
MARSHALL ALLEN

FLUTES
PAT PATRICK, DANNY DAVIS

BASS CLARINET
ROBERT CUMMINS

TROMBONE
ALI HARSAN

TENOR SAXOPHONE
JOHN GILMORE

BARITONE SAXOPHONE
PAT PATRICK

ALTO SAXOPHONE
MARSHALL ALLEN, DANNY DAVIS

BASS VIOL
RONNIE BOYKINS

LOG DRUMS
JAMES JACSON

The music-al progression of Sun Ra, has been the building-up of a Unit – The Arkestra, and to evolve this Unit through the Solar, Myth-Science, Astro-infinity Power, phases of Astro-infinity Music. This process of musical evolution has involved a calculated correlation of the Unit's musical growth/dimensions, with its size/musicians – instrumentation, and manipulating the Unit to ensure that any given time, it is performing/working at maximum output . . . Sustaining a continuous creative process, Growth, towards boundless infinity.

The inter-relation with/in and from the Unit; as terms of reference is Sound. And the first principle of the Unit has been to master Sound – the essence of music/magic, and to project pure sound – sound, as value, and as a manifestation of power/energy, pure and undefiled, with which to break/through the limitations of the word barrier, and move expression/communication into a no-man space of sound.

By vitalizing sound, making it come alive/vibrant as feelings/ideas, use music to replace word-language as the true medium for communication. For Sun Ra this has meant the use of music to communicate his message of co-awareness – beyond social consciousness into a higher and loner spiritual realm of potential being – dealt with on Other Planes of There – Saturn LP KH–98766.

This message is directed at what he calls the 'alter-self,' the potential, untouched/unaffected by environment/civilization.

"The Alter happiness
is not the reality
But the alter happiness is the myth.

From the realm of the myth comes the impossible
And the potentials of the impossible;"

His poem, Music, The Neglected Plane of Wisdom (1955) in which he states that 'Music is a plane of wisdom, because music is a universal language' . . . and 'Music is existence, the key to the universal language,' is his blueprint for the ideas which he re-translates into his music. His music is then 'the plane of wisdom, and a weapon of defense against the past and the condemnations of the past – the weapon with which he harmonizes the listener, the music is a sunburst of burning sounds. Natural, warm. Fire music.

The Myth-Science Arkestra was initiated to revive the whole spectrum of sounds, recreating the total Energy needed to restore the power of the ORIGINAL symbol – THE ANKHNATION.

These 'anthems' serve as mental therapy (Cosmic Tones for Mental Therapy – Saturn LP – Vol. II, 408) to negate time, and speed the mind towards recognizing the systems involved/used in the transfer from symbol to word; words having been twisted/lost their meaning and value. To get the mind away from the world-word-traps of Freedom, Love, Peace, and instead direct it into the depth/space of these sounds to investigate, search, and within them find meaning/being.

Through his music Sun Ra demonstrates the Energy of Unity, and by substituting interdependence for independence, discipline for freedom, prepares and directs existence towards other wordliness.

The theme song of the Myth-Science Arkestra, Interplanetary Music (Interstellar Low Ways – Saturn LP 203), advocates this direction . . . Interplanetary . . . Interplanetary Music. Interplanetary Melodies . . . Interplanetary Harmonies – the lyrics and the instrumentation – strings, horns, voices, pulsating as a combination of primitive/modern sounds, bridging the split between object and shadow; the two sides of a balanced Equation. On this record, the STRANGE STRINGS SOUND; STRINGS, instruments linking East and West – The Universe, are stretched, stroked, struck, bowed, plucked and picked to vibrate the air and radiate the rays of sounds in movements re-presenting Nature as Music.

Sun Ra and his tone-scientists/magicians, project these Voices-whispers, talking drums, thunder drums, to fill the Silence. And these SOUNDS, graduated on a relative Scale linking their quality to affect, halo-hang-like spells over the mind.

The music of the Myth-Science Arkestra is the music of illusion and wonder – A wonder-full music; the medium for the UNREAL and the UNSEEN . . . WORLDS APPROACHING.

The Solar Arkestra 'revealed' the Secrets of the Sun – Saturn LP 9954; The Magic City, and The Shadow World, as seen by The Abstract Eye and The Abstract I. – Saturn LP 403.
STRANGE STRINGS is 'The beginning of a series that would be a bridge to some and a wall to others that are not Nature-Sincere. Sincerity, is the only truth in tune with the greater being.'

TAM FIOFORI.

SUN RA and his ASTRO INFINITY ARKESTRA   STRANGE STRINGS   LP #5472

Recording Engineer: A. Abraham
Studio: EL SATURN
A product of Infinity, Inc. Chicago, Illinois

EL SATURN RECORDS
P.O. BOX 7124 - CHICAGO, ILLINOIS

Compositions and arrangements by SUN RA
Published by ENTERPLANETARY BMI copyright
Photo Art By CHARLES SHABACON

WE TRAVEL THE SPACE WAYS

SUN RA and his myth SCIENCE ARKESTRA

SUN RA and his myth SCIENCE ARKESTRA
"we travel the space ways"

SIDE A
INTERPLANETARY MUSIC
(VOCAL BY THE ARKESTRA)
• EVE
• WE TRAVEL THE SPACE WAYS
(VOCAL BY THE ARKESTRA)
• TAPESTRY FROM AN ASTEROID

SIDE B
• SPACE LONELINESS
• NEW HORIZONS
• VELVET

FEATURING

SUN RA, Piano, Electronic Piano, Cosmic Tone Organ
JOHN GILMORE, Tenor Bells
PAT PATRICK, Baritone Sax
MARSHALL ALLEN, Alto
RONNIE BOYKINS, Bass
WALTER STRICKLAND, Trumpet
ART HOYLE, Trumpet
PHIL CORHAN, Trumpet
NATE PRYOR, Trombone
JULIAN PRIESTER, Trombone
ROBERT BARRY, Percussion
EDWARD SKINNER, Percussion

PAT PATRICK   Photo Courtesy of ATRA Productions, Chicago, Ill.

INTERPLANETARY MUSIC, Sun Ra, Cosmic Tone Organ;
Vocal bythe Arkestra; Phil Corhan, Space Harp;
Ronnie Boykins, Bass; John Gilmore, Cosmic Bells.

EVE Walter Strickland, Trumpet; Sun Ra, Piano; Nate
Pryor, Trombone;

WE TRAVEL THE SPACE WAYS, Sun Ra, Piano; Vocal by
the Arkestra; Marshall Allen, Bells and Flying Saucer;
Ronnie Boykins, Bass.

TAPESTRY FROM AN ASTEROID, Phil Corhan, Trumpet;
John Gilmore Tenor.

SPACE LONELINESS, Sun Ra Piano; Walter Strickland,
Trumpet; Sun Ra, Piano; Marshall Allen, Alto.

NEW HORIZONS, Sun Ra, Piano; Arthur Hoyle, Trumpet;
Julian Priester, Trombone; John Gilmore, Bells.

VELVET, Phil Corhan, Trumpet; John Gilmore, Tenor;
Sun Ra, Piano; Marshall Allen, Alto.

Recording Engineer: A Abraham
Studio: EL SATURN
A Product of Infinity, Inc. Chicago, Illinois

SOLAR FIDELITY
LP # 409

EL SATURN RECORDS - P.O. BOX 7124 - CHICAGO, ILLINOIS

SUN RA and his MYTH-SCIENCE ARKESTRA

THE NUBIANS of PLUTONIA

SUN RA and his MYTH-SCIENCE ARKESTRA   **"THE NUBIANS OF PLUTONIA"**

FEATURING

SUN RA, Electronic Piano,
PAT PATRICK, Baritone Sax
RONNIE BOYKINS, Bass
CHARLES DAVIS, Baritone Sax
ROBERT BARRY, Percussion
NATE PRYOR, Trombone

JOHN GILMORE, Tenor Sax
MARSHALL ALLEN, Alto, Flute
JAMES SPAULDING, Alto Sax
LUCIOUS RANDOLPH, Trumpet
JIM HERNDON, Timbali
PHIL CORHAN, Trumpet

Recording Engineer: A. Abraham
Studio: EL SATURN

Cover Art: Richard Pedreguera
A Product of Infinity, Inc. Chicago, Illinois

SIDE A

PLUTONIAN NIGHTS

THE GOLDEN LADY

STAR TIME;

SIDE B

NUBIA

AFRICA

WATUSA

AIETHOPIA;

LP #406
Compositions and Arrangements by SUN RA
Published by ENTERPLANETARY—BMI ©

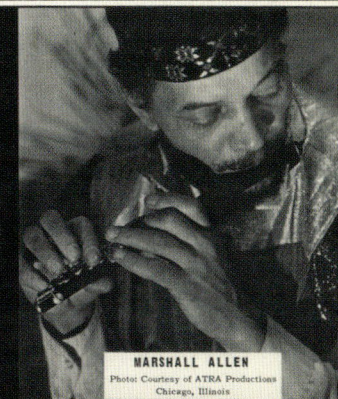

MARSHALL ALLEN
Photo Courtesy of ATRA Productions
Chicago, Illinois

PLUTONIAN NIGHTS, SUN RA, Piano; JOHN GILMORE,
Tenor; RONNIE BOYKINS, Bass.

THE GOLDEN LADY, SUN RA, Piano Electronic; JAMES
SPAULDING, Alto; MARSHALL ALLEN, Flute;
JAMES SPAULDING, Alto; MARSHALL ALLEN,
Flute; LUCIOUS RANDOLPH, Trumpet; ROBERT
BARRY, Percussion; JIM HERNDON, Percussion,
RONNIE BOYKINS, Bass.

STAR TIME, PAT PATRICK, Baritone Sax; JAMES
SPAULDING, Alto; NATE PRYOR, Trombone;
JOHN GILMORE, Tenor Sax.

NUBIA, SUN RA, Electronic Piano; ROBERT BARRY,
JIM HERNDON, Percussion; JOHN GILMORE,
Nigerian Bells.

AFRICA, Vocal performed by the Arkestra; MARSHALL
ALLEN, Flute.

WATUSA, RONNIE BOYKINS, Bass; SUN RA, Piano;
ROBERT BARRY, Percussion.

AIETHOPIA, SUN RA, Piano; MARSHALL ALLEN,
Flute; JIM HERNDON, Timbali; ROBERT BARRY,
Drums.

EL SATURN RECORDS - P.O. BOX 7124 - CHICAGO, ILLINOIS

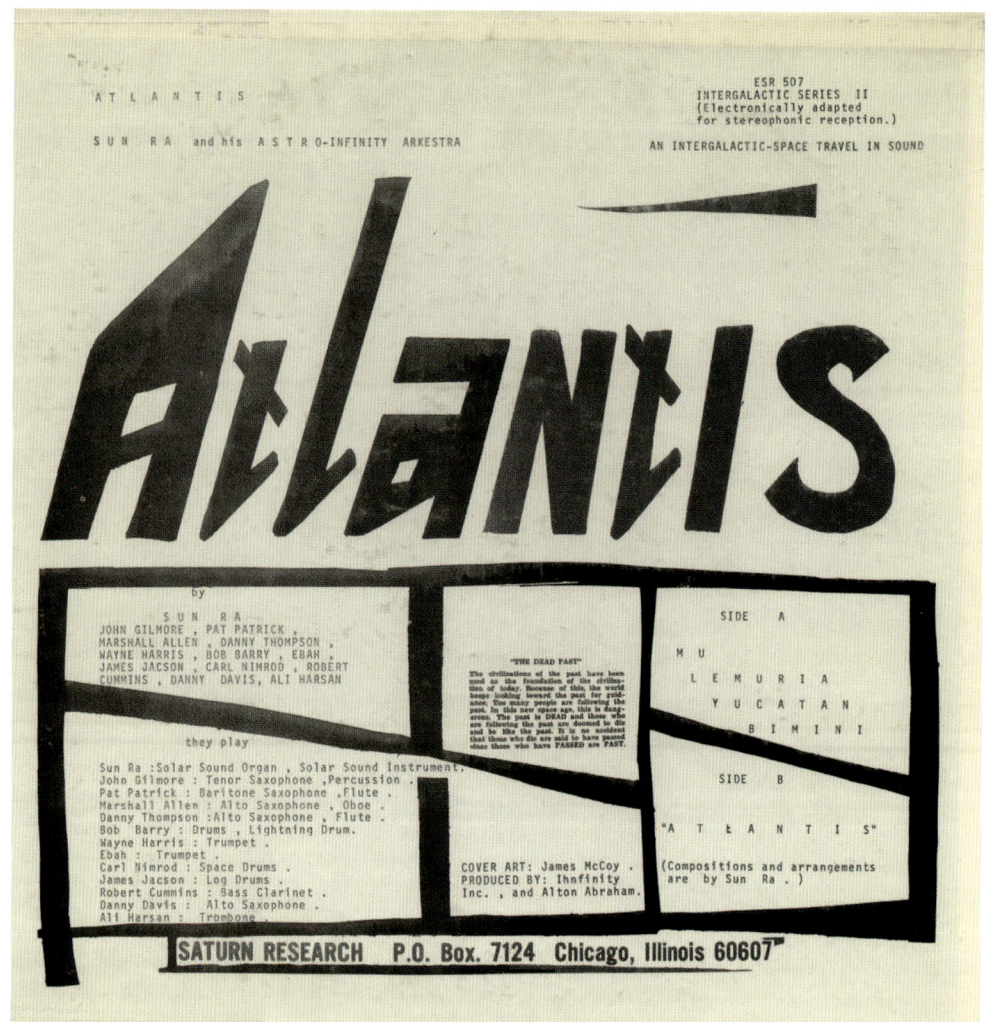

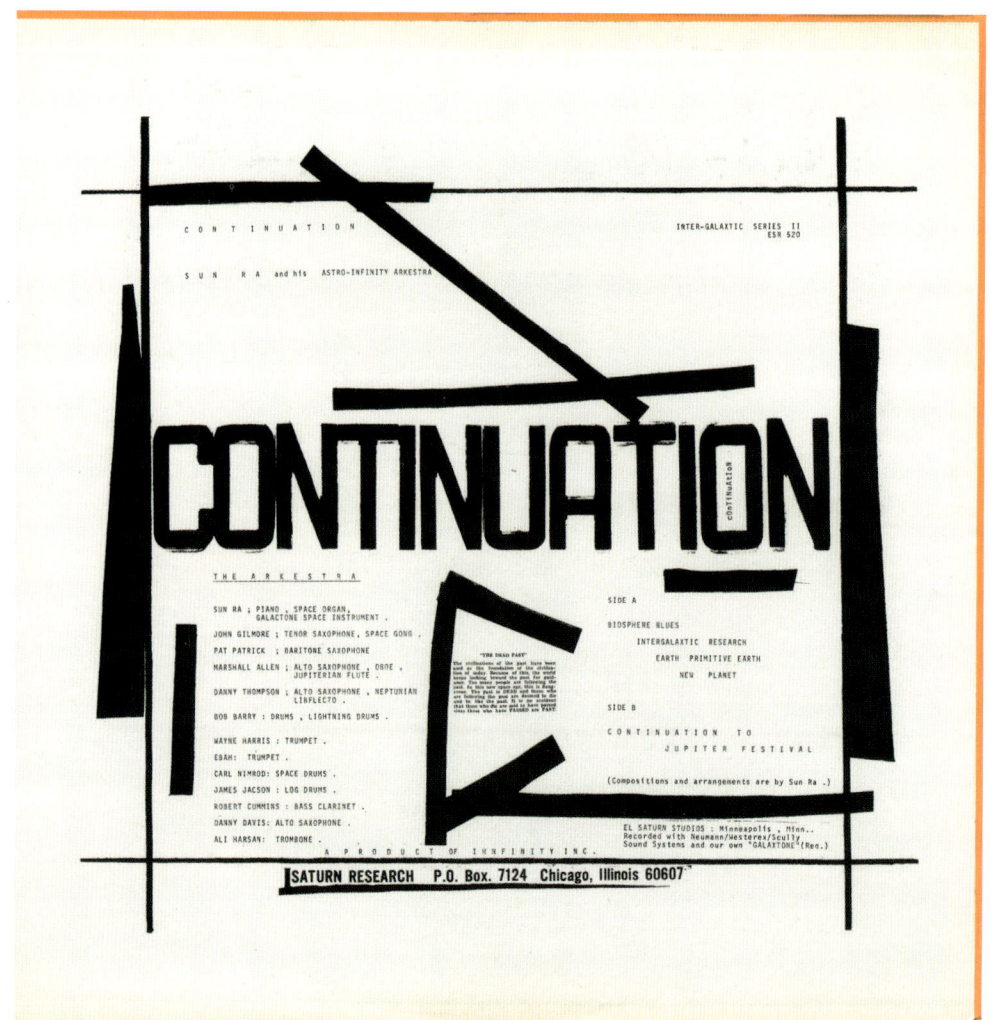

SUN-RA and his ASTRO INFINITY ARKESTRA

In Living Stereo SR 508-B

"HOLIDAY FOR SOUL DANCE"

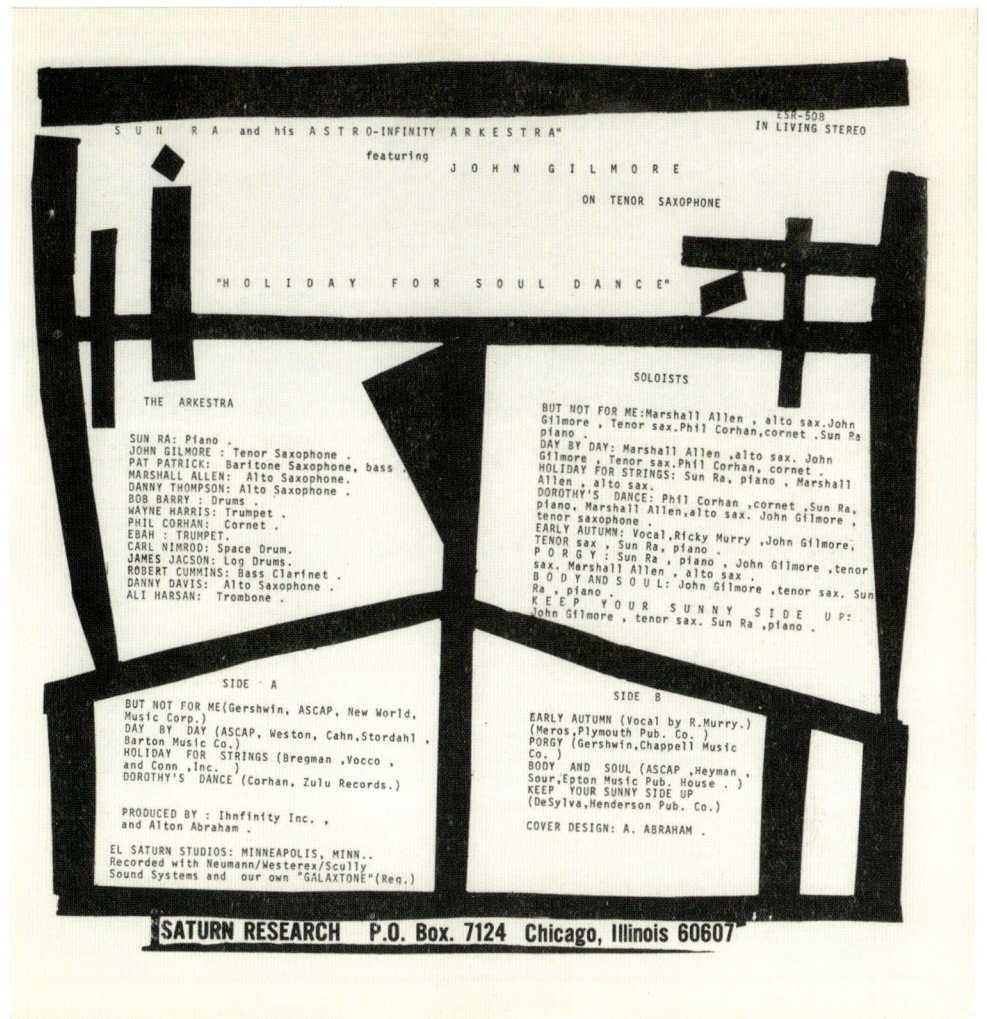

SUN RA and his ASTRO-INFINITY ARKESTRA"

featuring JOHN GILMORE ON TENOR SAXOPHONE

ESR-508 IN LIVING STEREO

"HOLIDAY FOR SOUL DANCE"

THE ARKESTRA

SUN RA : Piano .
JOHN GILMORE : Tenor Saxophone .
PAT PATRICK: Baritone Saxophone, bass
MARSHALL ALLEN: Alto Saxophone .
DANNY THOMPSON: Alto Saxophone .
BOB BARRY : Drums
WAYNE HARRIS: Trumpet .
PHIL CORHAN: Cornet .
EBAH : TRUMPET .
CARL NIMROD: Space Drum .
JAMES JACSON: Log Drums .
ROBERT CUMMINS: Bass Clarinet .
DANNY DAVIS: Alto Saxophone .
ALI HARSAN: Trombone .

SOLOISTS

BUT NOT FOR ME:Marshall Allen , alto sax.John Gilmore , Tenor sax.Phil Corhan,cornet ,Sun Ra piano .
DAY BY DAY: Marshall Allen ,alto sax. John Gilmore , Tenor sax.Phil Corhan, cornet , John .
HOLIDAY FOR STRINGS: Sun Ra , piano , Marshall Allen , alto sax.
DOROTHY'S DANCE: Phil Corhan ,cornet ,Sun Ra , piano, Marshall Allen,alto sax. John Gilmore , tenor saxophone .
EARLY AUTUMN: Vocal,Ricky Murry ,John Gilmore , TENOR sax , Sun Ra , piano .
P O R G Y : Sun Ra , piano , John Gilmore , tenor sax, Marshall Allen , alto sax .
B O D Y A N D S O U L: John Gilmore ,tenor sax. Sun Ra , piano .
K E E P Y O U R S U N N Y S I D E U P : John Gilmore , tenor sax. Sun Ra ,piano .

SIDE A

BUT NOT FOR ME(Gershwin, ASCAP, New World, Music Corp.)
DAY BY DAY (ASCAP, Weston, Cahn,Stordahl , Barton Music Co.)
HOLIDAY FOR STRINGS (Bregman ,Vocco , and Conn ,Inc.)
DOROTHY'S DANCE (Corhan, Zulu Records.)

PRODUCED BY : Ihnfinity Inc., and Alton Abraham .

EL SATURN STUDIOS: MINNEAPOLIS, MINN..
Recorded with Neumann/Westerex/Scully
Sound Systems and our own "GALAXTONE"(Reg.)

SIDE B

EARLY AUTUMN (Vocal by R.Murry.)
(Meros ,Plymouth Pub. Co.)
PORGY (Gershwin,Chappell Music Co.)
BODY AND SOUL (ASCAP ,Heyman , Sour,Epton Music Pub. House .)
KEEP YOUR SUNNY SIDE UP (DeSylva,Henderson Pub.Co.)

COVER DESIGN : A. ABRAHAM .

SATURN RESEARCH   P.O. Box 7124 Chicago, Illinois 60607

LIVING STEREO

"THE NIGHT OF THE PURPLE MOON"

Sun Ra

AND HIS INTERGALACTIC INFINITY ARKESTRA

IR522

INTERGALACTIC II IR522
LIVING STEREO

Sun Ra AND HIS INTERGALACTIC INFINITY ARKESTRA

"THE NIGHT OF THE PURPLE MOON"

PARALLELS

IF IT IS NOT HERE
IT MUST BE THERE
FOR SOMEWHERE AND NOWHERE
PARALLELS
IN VERSIONS OF EACH OTHER ....WHERE
NOTHING AFTER SOMETHING IS NOT
OR EVEN BEFORE SOMETHING CAME TO BE

RA

THE ARKESTRA

SUN RA: TWO MOOG SYNTHESIZERS, ROKSICHORD.

JOHN GILMORE: TENOR SAX, PERCUSSION.

DANNY DAVIS: ALTO SAX, CLARINET.

STAFFORD JAMES: ELECTRONIC BASS

SUN RA: Plays MOOG SYNTHESIZERS and ROKSICHORD on Blue Soul, Narrative and Outside The Time Zone. He plays the ROKSICHORD on the remaining songs.

JOHN GILMORE: Plays PERCUSSION on all songs except Impromptu Festival. HE plays TENOR SAX on Impromptu Festival.

DANNY DAVIS: Plays DRUMS on Impromptu Festival.

SIDE A

SUN-EARTH ROCK   4:37
THE ALL OF EVERYTHING   4:22
IMPROMPTU FESTIVAL   4:00
BLUE SOUL   3:44
NARRATIVE   2:53
OUTSIDE THE TIME ZONE   5:00

SIDE B

THE NIGHT OF THE PURPLE MOON   3:45
A BIRD'S EYE-VIEW OF MAN'S WORLD   2:56
21ST CENTURY ROMANCE   4:05
DANCE OF THE LIVING IMAGE   4:35
LOVE IN OUTER SPACE   3:45

(Compositions and arrangements are by Sun Ra.)

CO-PRODUCERS: IHNFINITY INC./T.S. MIMS.

EL SATURN RESEARCH   P.O. Box 7124 Chicago, Illinois 60607

SUN-RA — MY BROTHER THE WIND
and his
ASTRO INFINITY ARKESTRA

INTERGALACTIC SERIES II
"MY BROTHER THE WIND"
STEREO
ESRS21
AN INTERGALACTIC-SPACE TRAVEL IN SOUND

MY BROTHER THE WIND

SUN RA AND HIS ASTRO-SOLAR INFINITY ARKESTRA

featuring JOHN GILMORE, on Percussion

THE DIFFERENCES

SIDE A
MY BROTHER THE WIND
INTERGALACTIC II
TO NATURE'S GOD

SOMETIMES IN THE AMAZING IGNORANCE
I HEAR THINGS AND SEE THINGS
I NEVER KNEW I SAW AND HEARD BEFORE
SOMETIMES IN THE IGNORANCE
I FEEL THE MEANING
INVINCIBLE, INVISIBLE WISDOM
AND I COMMUNE WITH INTUITIVE INSTINCT
WITH THE FORCE THAT MADE LIFE BE
AND SINCE IT MADE LIFE BE
IT IS GREATER THAN LIFE
AND SINCE IT LET EXTINCTION BE
IT IS GREATER THAN EXTINCTION

I COMMUNE WITH FEELING MORE THAN
        PRAYER
FOR THERE IS NOTHING ELSE TO ASK FOR
THAT COMPANIONSHIP IS
AND IT IS SUPERIOR TO ANY OTHER IS

SIDE B
THE CODE OF INTERDEPENDENCE

SOMETIMES IN MY AMAZING IGNORANCE
OTHERS SEE ME ONLY AS THEY CARE TO SEE
I AM TO THEM AS THEY THINK
ACCORDING TO STANDARDS I SHOULD NOT BE
AND THAT IS THE DIFFERENCE BETWEEN I AND THEM
BECAUSE I SEE THEM AS THEY ARE TO IS
AND NOT THE SEEMING IGNORANCE OF THE WAS

RA

THE ARKESTRA

SUN RA: two moog synthesizers.
JOHN GILMORE: tenor sax, percussion.
MARSHALL ALLEN: oboe, piccolo, flute
DANNY DAVIS: alto sax, clarinet.

"Beta Music for Beta People for a Beta World"

CO-PRODUCERS: IHNFINITY INC./T.S. MIMS

(Compositions and arrangements are by Sun Ra.)

SATURN RESEARCH P.O. Box 7124 Chicago, Illinois 60607

SUN-RA — MY BROTHER THE WIND
and his
ASTRO INFINITY ARKESTRA

THE WIND SPEAKS

Sun Ra AND HIS INTERGALACTIC INFINITY ARKESTRA

INTERGALACTIC II
LIVING STEREO
523
SRA 2000

AN INTERGALACTIC-SPACE TRAVEL IN SOUND

MY BROTHER THE WIND VOL. II

Featuring: ... SUN RA on MOOG SYNTHESIZER;
JUNE TYSON, Vocalist; JOHN GILMORE, Tenor Sax; KWAME HARDI, Trumpet;
PAT PATRICK, Baritone Sax; JAMES JACSON, Oboe.

THE ARKESTRA

JOHN GILMORE	Tenor, percussion
PAT PATRICK	Baritone sax
MARSHALL ALLEN	Alto sax, flute
DANNY THOMPSON	Baritone sax
DANNY DAVIS	Alto sax
JAMES JACSON	Oboe, drums
NIMROD	Drums
WILLIAM BRISTER	Drums
AHKTAL EBAH	Trumpet
KWAME HARDI	Trumpet
LEX HUMPHRIES	Drums
ALEXANDER BLAKE	Bass
ROBERT CUMMINGS	Drums
SUN RA	MOOG, Intergalactic Organ

SIDE A	SIDE B
SOMEWHERE ELSE	OTHERNESS BLUE
CONTRAST	SOMEBODY ELSE'S WORLD
THE WIND SPEAKS	PLEASANT TWILIGHT
SUN THOUGHTS	WALKING ON THE MOON
JOURNEY TO THE STARS	
WORLD OF THE MYTH "I"	
THE DESIGN-COSMOS II	

(Compositions and arrangements are by SUN RA)

OTHER ALBUMS BY THE SUN RA ARKESTRA

"FATE IN A PLEASANT MOOD"	"JAZZ IN SILHOUETTE"
"COSMIC TONES FOR MENTAL THERAPY"	"SUPERSONIC JAZZ"
"MAGIC CITY"	"MONORAILS AND SATELLITES" VOL. I
"THE NUBIANS OF PLUTONIA"	"MONORAILS AND SATELLITES" VOL. II
"STRANGE STRINGS"	"THE NIGHT OF THE PURPLE MOON"
"SECRETS OF THE SUN"	"MY BROTHER THE WIND" VOL. I
"CONTINUATION TO"	"MY BROTHER THE WIND" VOL. II
"ARTFORMS FROM DIMENSIONS TOMORROW"	"ATLANTIS"
"INTERSTELLAR LOW WAYS"	"HOLIDAY FOR SOUL DANCE"
"ANGELS AND DEMONS AT PLAY"	"OTHER PLANES OF THERE"

AND OTHERS, WRITE:

PRODUCER: IHNFINITY INC.

EL SATURN RESEARCH P.O. Box 7124 Chicago, Illinois 60607

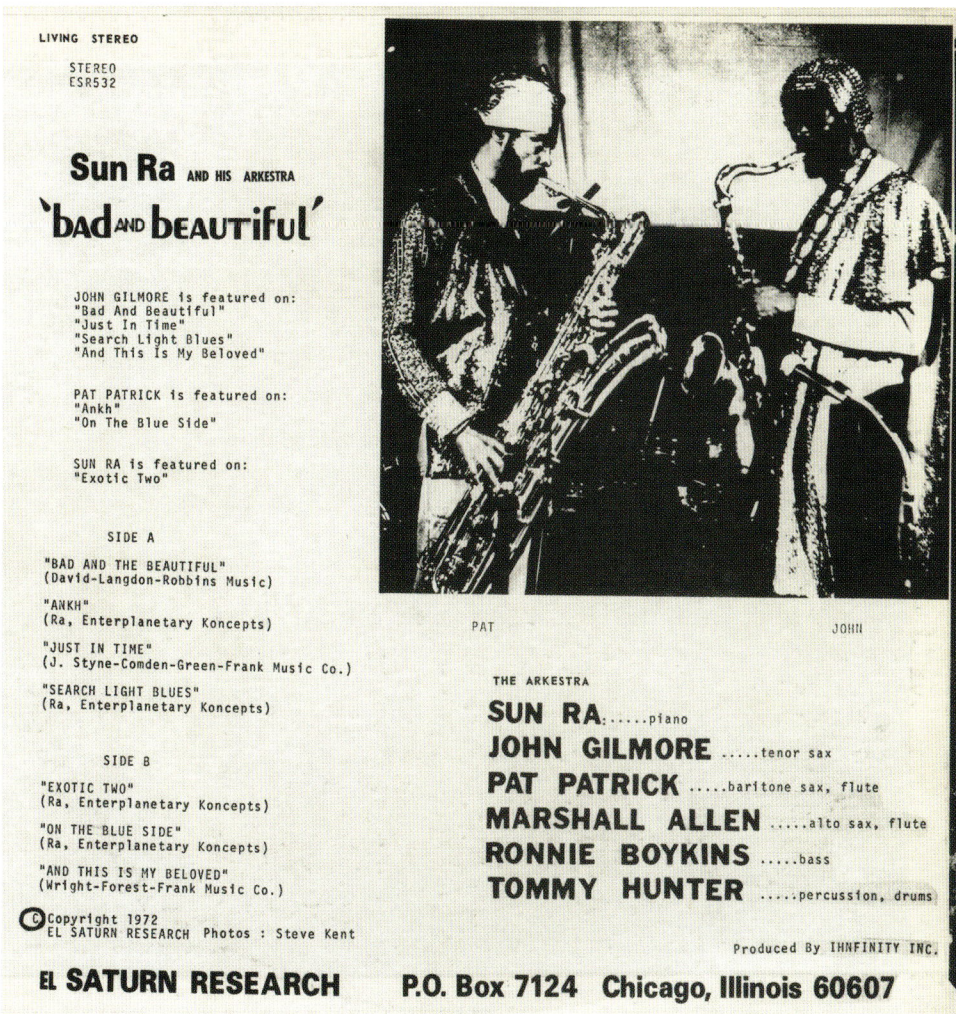

SATURN
℗ 1979
101679B
SIDE B
SUN
33 1/3 RPM
enterplan
bmi
SEDUCTIVE FANTASY
(RA)

enterplan
bmi
SIDE #1
V-EDITION
142000 A
OTHERNESS BLUE
SOMEBODY ELSE'S IDEA
PLEASANT TWILIGHT
WALKIN' ON THE MOON
(RA)
℗ 1978 SATURN

RA
enterplan:
bmi
THE SOUND MIRROR
(RA)
℗ 1970 SATURN
2-A

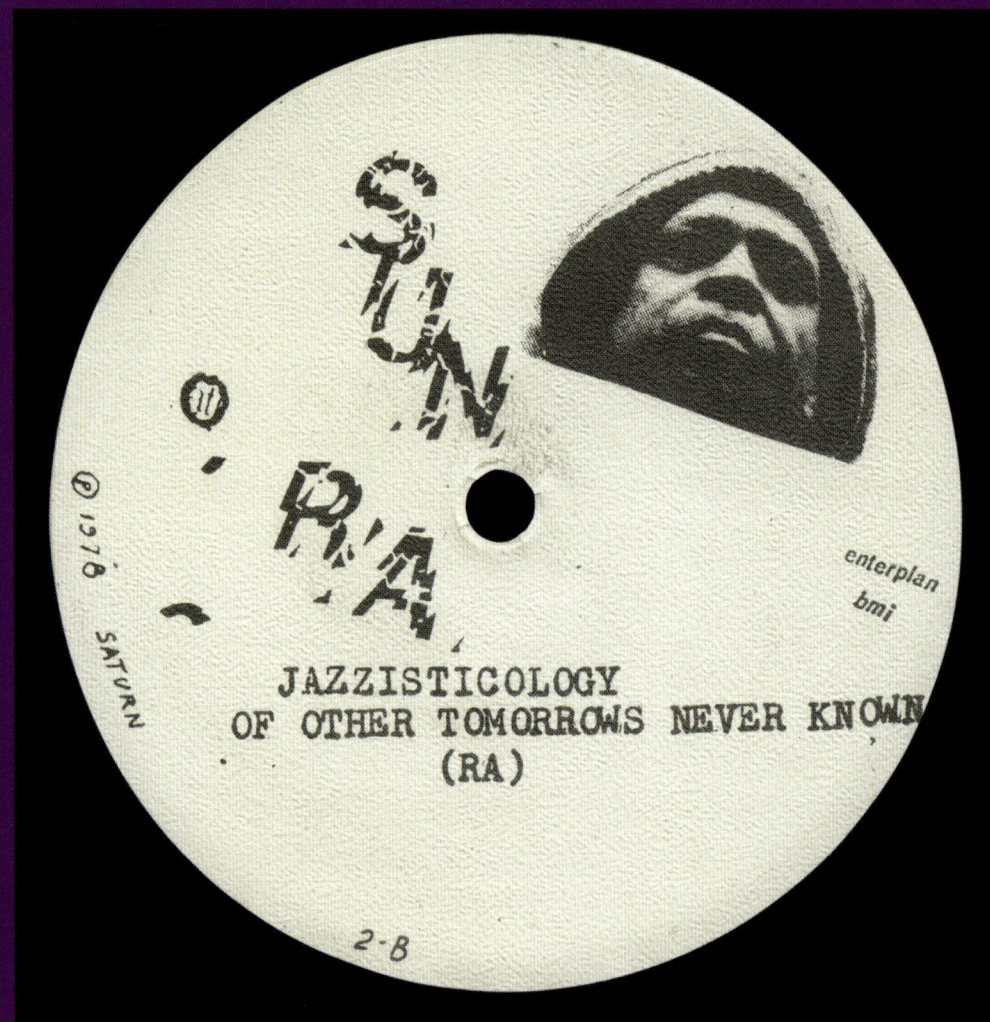

SUN RA
℗ 1978 SATURN
enterplan
bmi
JAZZISTICOLOGY
OF OTHER TOMORROWS NEVER KNOWN
(RA)
2-B

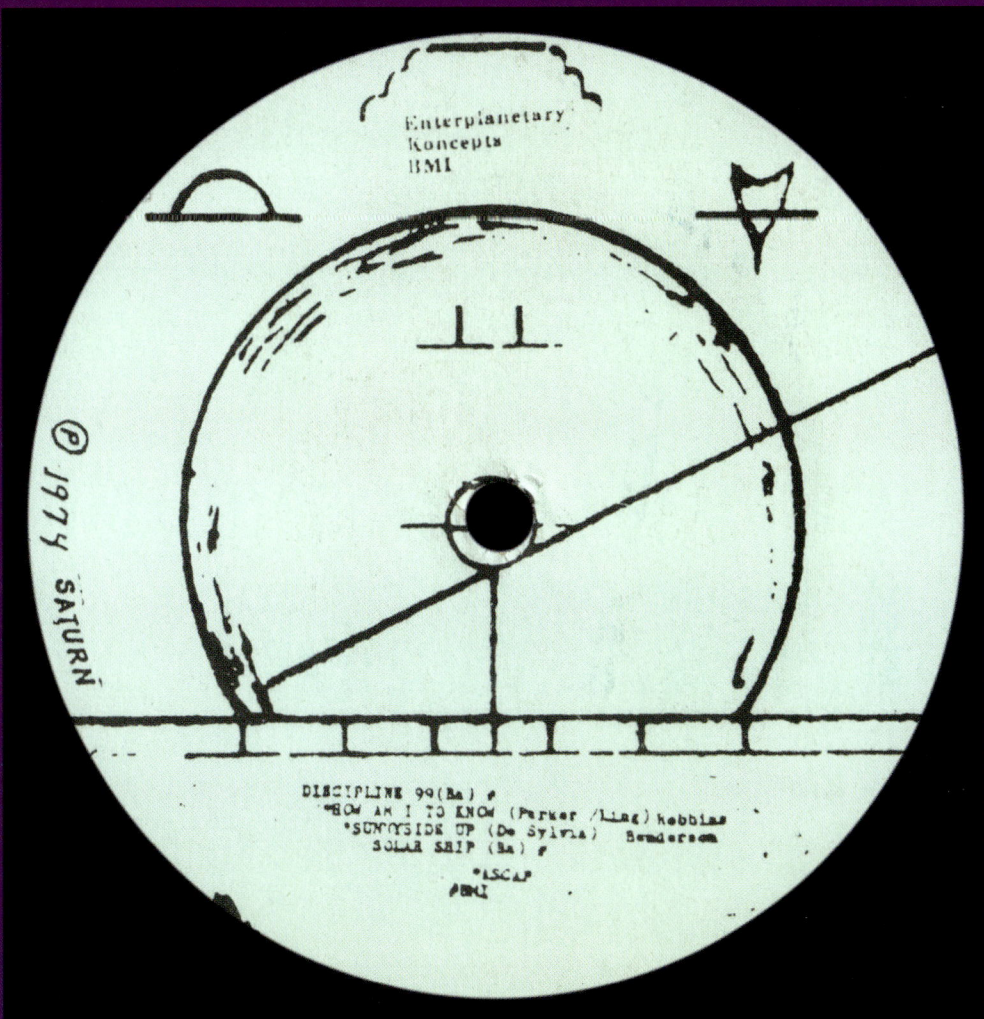

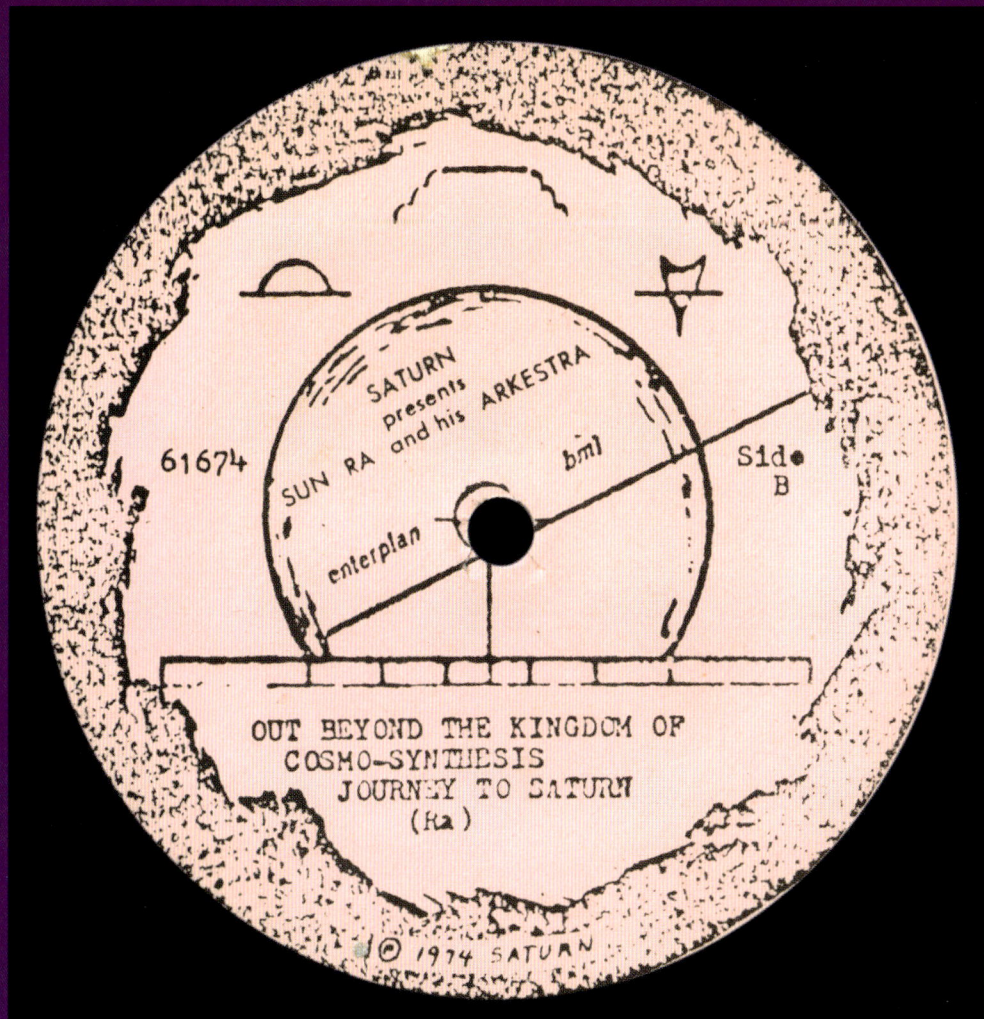

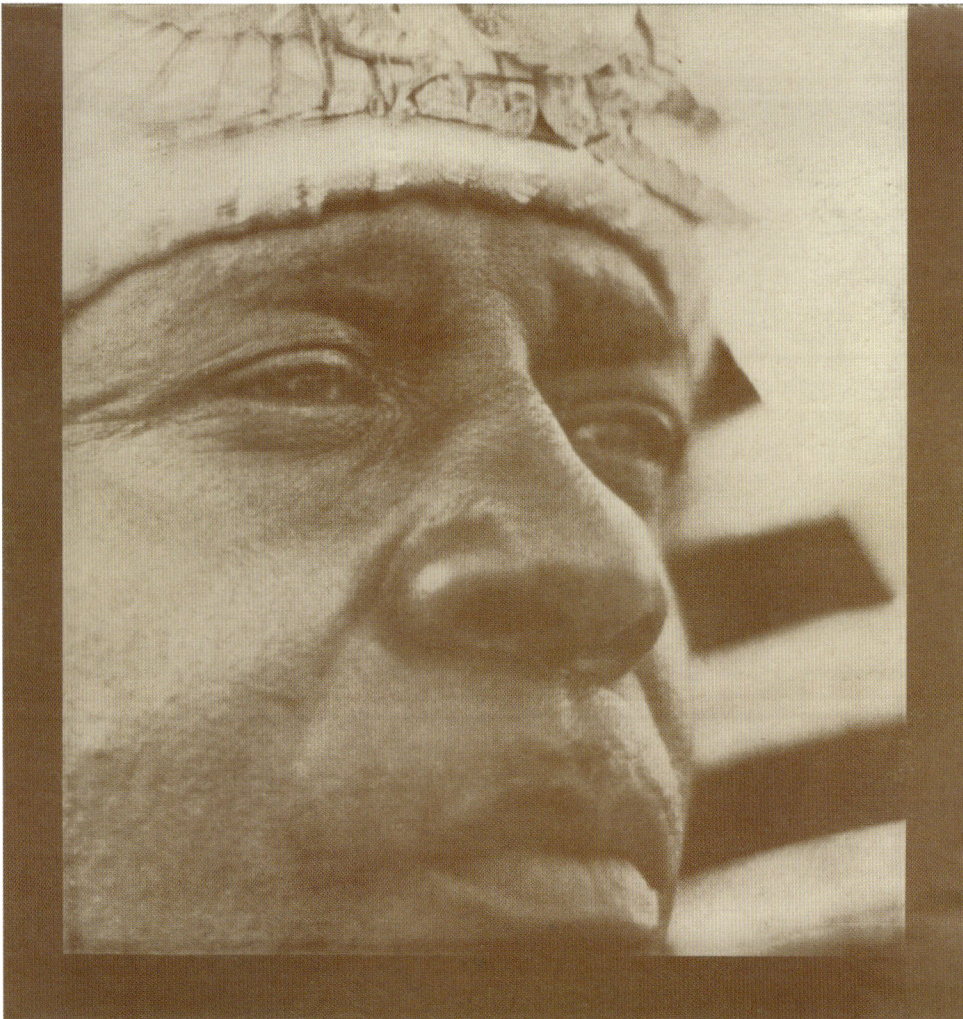

nidhamu

THE OUTER BRIDGE

In the half-between world
Dwell they the tone-scientists
Sound
Mathematically precise
They speak of many things
The sound-scientists
Architects of planes of discipline.

......Sun Ra

JOHN GILMORE– tenor saxophone, Percussion
DANNY DAVIS – Alto Saxophone, Flute
MARSHALL ALLEN – Alto Saxophone, Flute, Oboe
KWAME HADI – trumpet, Congo Drums
PAT PATRICK – baritone saxophone
ELO OMOE – Bass Clarinet
TOMMY HUNTER – Percussion
DANNY THOMPSON – Baritone Saxophone and Flute
JUNE TYSON – Vocal
LARRY NARTHINGTON – Alto Saxophone, Conga Drums
LEX HUMPHRIES – percussion
HAKIM RAHIM – alto saxophone, Flute
SUN RA – organ, moog, rockichord, piano

Recorded in Egypt

TAM FIOFORI – recording engineer
Photograph by SAM BANKHEAD
Liner Photo By MIKE EVANS
Produced by IHNFINITY INC and the EAST

sun ra in egypt

JOHN GILMORE – tenor saxophone, Percussion
DANNY DAVIS – Alto Saxophone, Flute
MARSHALL ALLEN – Alto Saxophone, Flute, Oboe
KWAME HADI – trumpet, Congo Drums
PAT PATRICK – baritone saxophone
ELO OMOE – Bass Clarinet
TOMMY HUNTER – Percussion
DANNY THOMPSON – Baritone Saxophone and Flute
JUNE TYSON – Vocal
LARRY NARTHINGTON – Alto Saxophone, Conga Drums
LEX HUMPHRIES – percussion
HAKIM RAHIM – alto saxophone, Flute
SUN RA – organ, moog, rockichord, piano

Recorded in Egypt

TAM FIOFORI – recording engineer
Photograph by SAM BANKHEAD
Produced by IHNFINITY INC. and the EAST

"dark myth equation visitation"

Anything can give up it's life,
Why don't you give up your death?
Why don't you do something different
Something that was never done before?
So the universe will know you're here
So you can stand and speak to the universe
And say "Here I am!"
I am just like you:
Endless, Immeasurable, Eternal, Impossible

The universe has shown you the way

Go out look at the stars
They're always around
Go out and look at the sky
It's always there
Go out and look at the sun
In the morning
It's always here
Why do you have to go?
Why should you leave the stars
And the sun and the moon
And the universe all alone?

SUN RA ''Discipline 27-II''

DISCIPLINE SERIES.
From Secrets Of The Sun, Volume II.

THE ARKESTRA

JOHN GILMORE, Tenor sax, percussion.
MARSHALL ALLEN, Alto sax, flute.
DANNY DAVIS, Alto sax, flute.
PAT PATRICK, Baritone sax, bass.
DANNY THOMPSON, Baritone sax, flute.
KWAME HADI, Trumpet, bells, conga.
ELOE OMOE, Bass clarinet, flute.
AKH TAL EBAH, Trumpet, flugel horn.
LEX HUMPHRIES, Drums.
AL ZO WRIGHT, Drums.
HARRY RICHARDS, Drums.
ROBERT UNDERWOOD, Drums.
ATAKATUN, Conga.
STANLEY MORGAN, Conga.
ODUN, Conga.
RUSSELL BRANCH, Conga.
SUN RA; Electronic keyboard space age instruments,
moog, vocal dramatizing.

SPACE ETHNIC VOICES

JUNE TYSON
RUTH WRIGHT
JUDITH HOLTON
CHERYL BANKS
AKH TAL EBAH

SIDE ONE

PAN AFRO (8:02)
DISCIPLINE 8 (7:56)
NEPTUNE (5:47)

SIDE TWO

DISCIPLINE 27-II (24:29)

PAN AFRO
John Gilmore, tenor sax; Akh Tal Ebah, trumpet; Kwame Hadi, trumpet;
Sun Ra, space organ; Danny Davis, alto sax; Pat Patrick, bass.

DISCIPLINE 8
Sun Ra, space organ; Akh Tal Ebah, flugel horn; Marshall Allen, alto sax;
Danny Davis, alto sax; Eloe Omoe, bass clarinet; John Gilmore, tenor sax;
Stanley Morgan, Atakatun, Odun, Russel Branch, congas.

NEPTUNE
Sun Ra, space organ; Danny Thompson, baritone sax; Danny Davis, alto sax;
Akh Tal Ebah, flugel horn; Kwame Hadi, trumpet. Space Ethnic Voices:
June Tyson, John Gilmore, Akh Tal Ebah.

DISCIPLINE 27-II
The Voices of Sun Ra, June Tyson, Ruth Wright, Cheryl Banks, Judith Holton;
Kwame Hadi and Akh Tal Ebah, trumpet; Marshall Allen, alto sax.

PRODUCER: Alton Abraham and Ihnfinity Inc.

COVER ART: LeRoy Butler

Compositions and arrangements are by Sun Ra.

(P) 1973 SATURN RESEARCH

Poem taken from book titled "The Immeasurable Equation", by Sun Ra.
Book may be purchased through El Saturn Research.

EL SATURN RESEARCH
P.O. Box 7124
Chicago, Il. 60607

Sunbursts appear in dark disguises
Bringing to fore
The strange truth of Eternal myth
Is the Sound; It is the
Sound truth . . . Music Sound
And there always is music
The music always is
Whatever is
Always whatever is the music is
The sound pure
The sound symmetry
Equational values: vibrational
Differentiations: rhythms,
Harmonies, thought moods, Pattern
Silences that speak
Cohesive points bridges connect
opposites . . . . . .
There is black sound
The code
Projection sensitivity
Force reach decision
Perpendicular spirals
Galaxies, planets, earth
Man and his world
And the other world of man
Comprehension response
To the world of angels

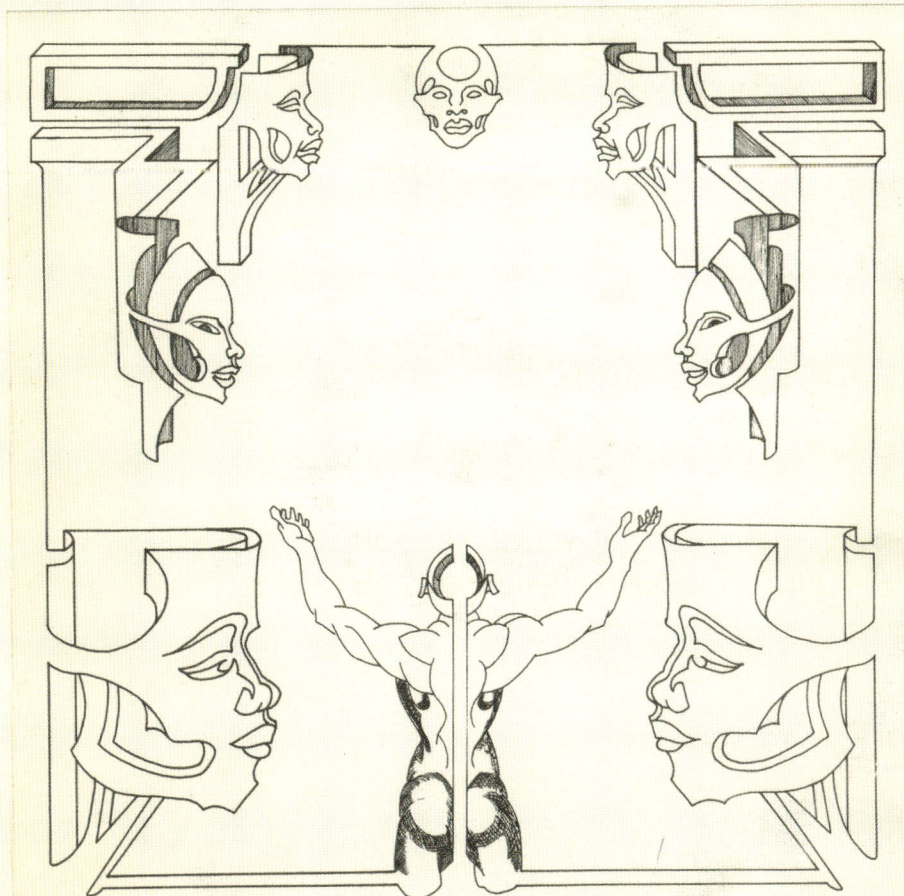

SUN RA

SUN RA AND HIS ARKESTRA

Featuring:
"SUN RA on PIANO"
AND
"JOHN GILMORE on TENOR SAX"

PLAYS

"A TONAL VIEW OF TIMES TOMORROW"

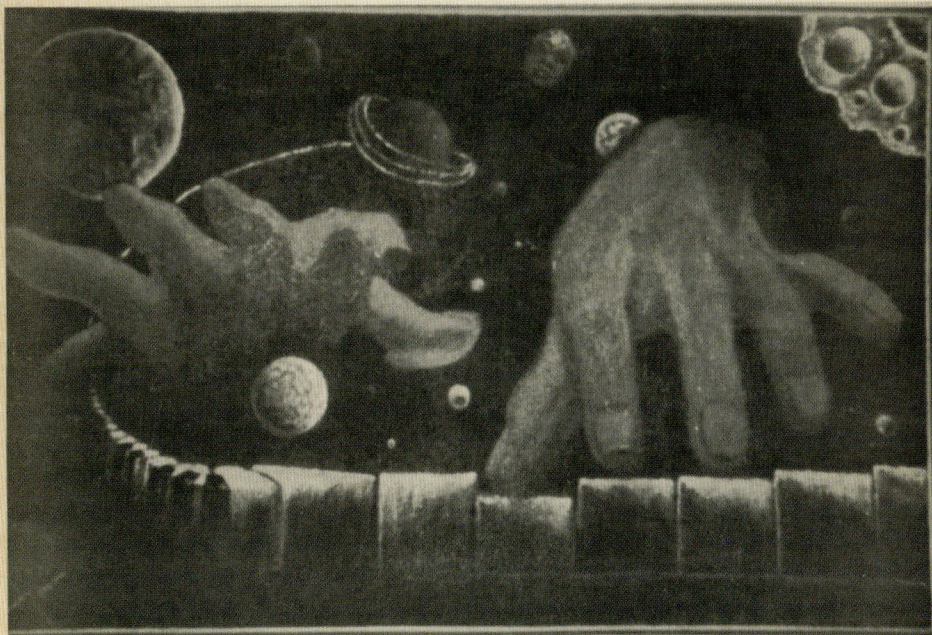

SUN-RA "MONORAILS AND SATELLITES" PLAYING
AT THE PIANO

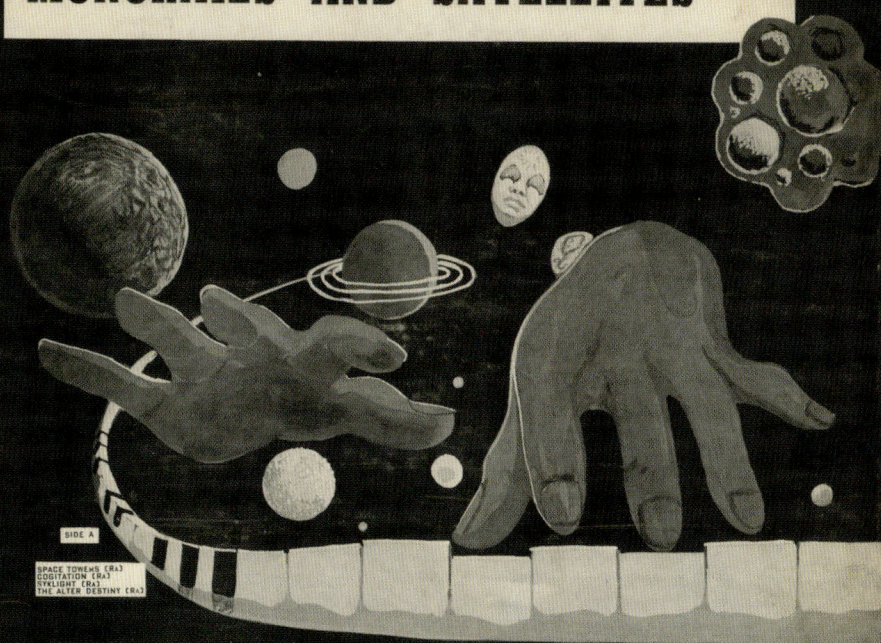

"MONORAILS AND SATELLITES" SR-509
33⅓ RPM

SIDE A
SPACE TOWERS (Ra)
COGITATION (Ra)
SKYLIGHT (Ra)
THE ALTER DESTINY (Ra)

SIDE B
EASY STREET
(Leeds Music, Hansen Pub. Co.)
BLUE DIFFERENTIALS (Ra)
MONORAILS AND SATELLITES (Ra)
THE GALAXY WAY (Ra)

COVER ART: RUDY IRVIN
PRODUCED BY: IHNFINITY INC. AND
ALTON ABRAHAM.

EL SATURN RECORDS   P.O. BOX 7124   CHICAGO, ILLINOIS

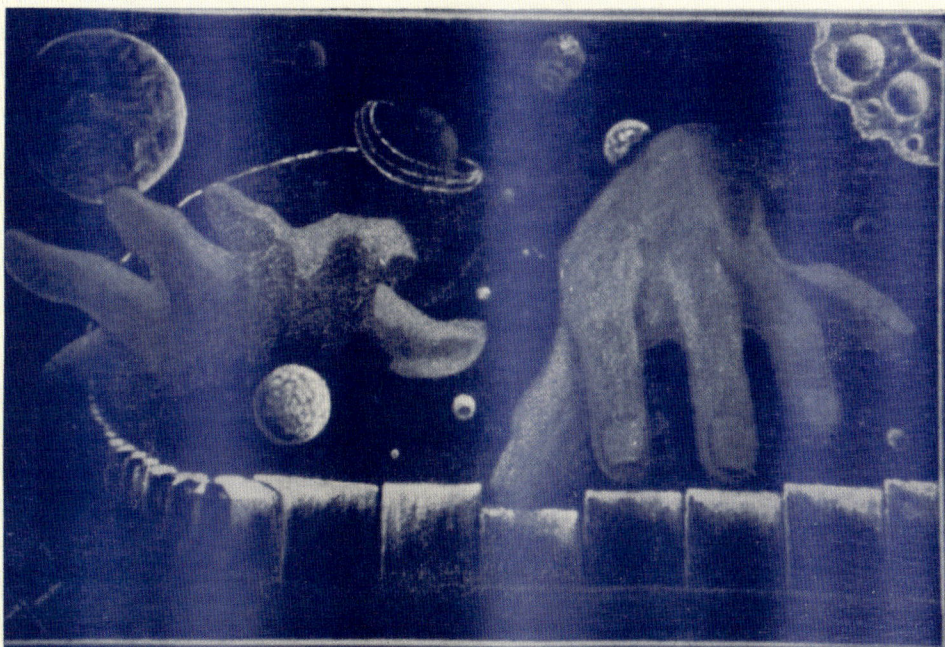

SUN-RA PLAYING
AT THE PIANO **MONORAILS & SATELLITES**

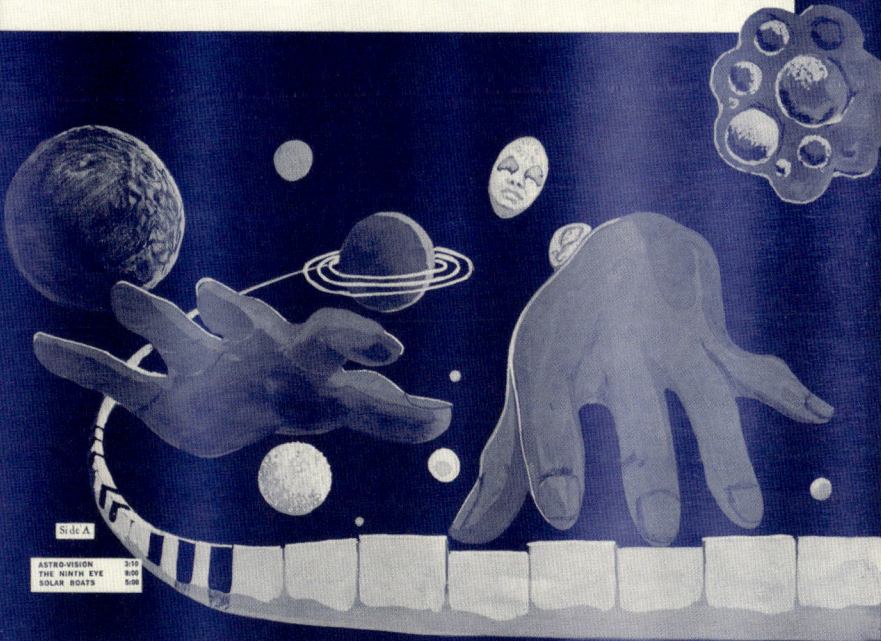

"MONORAILS AND SATELLITES" VOL. II
519
ESR-9691

Side A
ASTRO-VISION   3:10
THE NINTH EYE   8:00
SOLAR BOATS   5:00

SIDE B
Perspective Prisms of IS   6:20
Calundronius   8:00

PRODUCED BY: IHNFINITY INC. AND
ALTON ABRAHAM.
COVER ART: RUDY IRVIN
(Compositions and Arrangements
are by: Sun Ra)

EL SATURN RECORDS   P.O. BOX 7124   CHICAGO, ILLINOIS

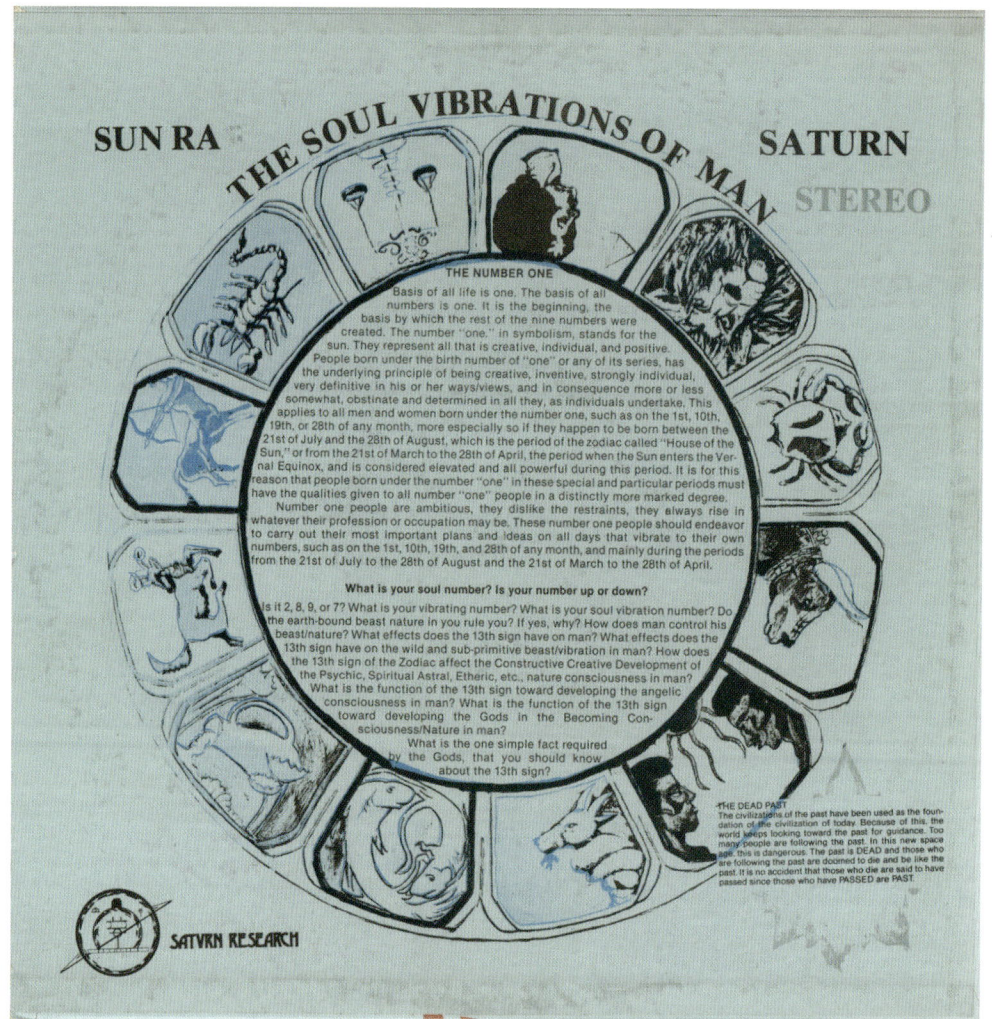

THE NUMBER ONE

Basis of all life is one. The basis of all numbers is one. It is the beginning, the basis by which the rest of the nine numbers were created. The number "one," in symbolism, stands for the sun. They represent all that is creative, individual, and positive.

People born under the birth number of "one" or any of its series, has the underlying principle of being creative, inventive, strongly individual, very definitive in his or her ways/views, and in consequence more or less somewhat, obstinate and determined in all they, as individuals undertake. This applies to all men and women born under the number one, such as on the 1st, 10th, 19th, or 28th of any month, more especially so if they happen to be born between the 21st of July and the 28th of August, which is the period of the zodiac called "House of the Sun," or from the 21st of March to the 28th of April, the period when the Sun enters the Vernal Equinox, and is considered elevated and all powerful during this period. It is for this reason that people born under the number "one" in these special and particular periods must have the qualities given to all number "one" people in a distinctly more marked degree.

Number one people are ambitious, they dislike the restraints, they always rise in whatever their profession or occupation may be. These number one people should endeavor to carry out their most important plans and ideas on all days that vibrate to their own numbers, such as on the 1st, 10th, 19th, and 28th of any month, and mainly during the periods from the 21st of July to the 28th of August and the 21st of March to the 28th of April.

What is your soul number? Is your number up or down?

Is it 2, 8, 9, or 7? What is your vibrating number? What is your soul vibration number? Do the earth-bound beast nature in you rule you? If yes, why? How does man control his beast/nature? What effects does the 13th sign have on man? What effects does the 13th sign have on the wild and sub-primitive beast/vibration in man? How does the 13th sign of the Zodiac affect the Constructive Creative Development of the Psychic, Spiritual Astral, Etheric, etc., nature consciousness in man? What is the function of the 13th sign toward developing the angelic consciousness in man? What is the function of the 13th sign toward developing the Gods in the Becoming Consciousness/Nature in man?

What is the one simple fact required by the Gods, that you should know about the 13th sign?

THE DEAD PAST

The civilizations of the past have been used as the foundation of the civilization of today. Because of this, the world keeps looking toward the past for guidance. Too many people are following the past. In this new space age, this is dangerous. The past is DEAD and those who are following the past are doomed to die and be like the past. It is no accident that those who die are said to have passed since those who have PASSED are PAST.

SATVRN RESEARCH

54

"STRANGE STRINGS"

SUN RA
℗ 1979 91379B
SIDE B
33 1/3 RPM
enterplan
bmi
OMNIVERSE
(RA)
VISITANT OF THE NINTH ULTIMATE
(RA)

SATURN
91379 A
33 1/3 RPM
enterplan
BMI
THE PLACE OF FIVE POINTS
WEST END SIDE OF MAGIC CITY
DARK LIGHTS IN A WHITE FOREST
(Compositions and Arrangements
By Sun Ra)
SATURN
5626 MORTON ST.
PHILADELPHIA, PA. 19144

SATURN
91379 B
33 1/3 RPM
enterplan
BMI
OMNIVERSE
VISITANT OF THE NINTH ULTIMATE
(Compositions and Arrangements
By Sun Ra)
SATURN
5626 MORTON ST.
PHILADELPHIA, PA. 19144

SUN RA
and HIS ARKESTRA
℗ 1979 SATURN
enterplan
bmi
101679A
33 1/3 RPM
ON JUPITER
(RA)
UFO
(RA, CLARKE, RICHARDSON)
SATURN P.O. BOX 7124 CHICAGO, ILLINOIS 60607

SATURN
℗ 1979 SATURN
101679B
33 1/3 RPM
enterplan
bmi
SEDUCTIVE FANTASY
(RA)
P.O. BOX 7124 CHICAGO, ILLINOIS 60607

SATURN
presents
SUN RA and his
INTERGALACTIC RESEARCH ARKESTRA
℗ 1974
61674 A
STEREO
33 1/3 RPM
1. DISCIPLINE 99 (RA)
   (Enterplane Publishers BMI)
2. HOW AM I TO KNOW (Parker & King)
   Robbins Music
3. SUNNYSIDE UP (De Sylvia)
   Henderson Publishers
4. SOLAR SHIP (RA)
   (Enterplane Publishers BMI)
(compositions and arrangements
by Sun Ra)
Enterplanetary
Koncepts
BMI
SATURN
5626 MORTON ST
PHILADELPHIA, PA. 19144

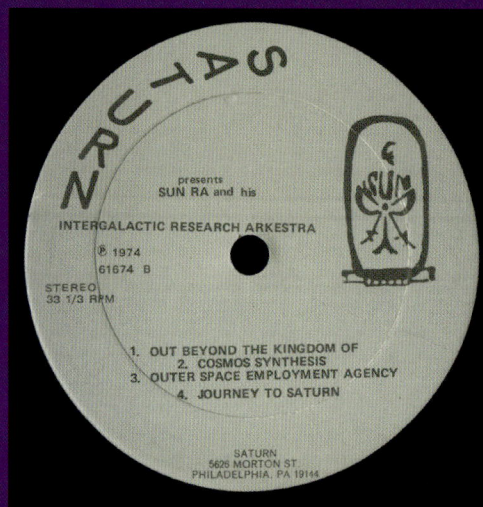

SATURN
presents
SUN RA and his
INTERGALACTIC RESEARCH ARKESTRA
℗ 1974
61674 B
STEREO
33 1/3 RPM
1. OUT BEYOND THE KINGDOM OF
2. COSMOS SYNTHESIS
3. OUTER SPACE EMPLOYMENT AGENCY
4. JOURNEY TO SATURN
SATURN
5626 MORTON ST
PHILADELPHIA, PA. 19144

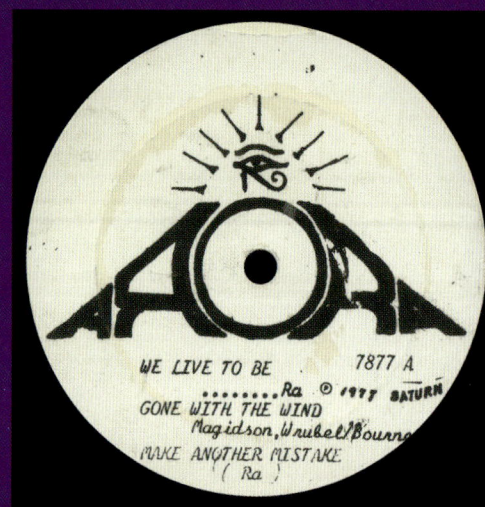

AURA
.........Ra ℗ 1977 SATURN
WE LIVE TO BE
7877 A
GONE WITH THE WIND
Magidson, Wrubel, Bourne
MAKE ANOTHER MISTAKE
(Ra)

EL SATURN
presents
SUN RA
and his ARKESTRA
Playing
"TAKING A CHANCE ON CHANCES"
LONG PLAY
33/3RPM
SIDE A
772-A
STEREO
℗ © 1977
enterplan
bmi
TAKING A CHANCE ON CHANCES
(Sun Ra; BMI: ENTERPLANETARY KONCEPTS)
LADY BIRD
(L. Hazelwood; ASCAP; L. Hazelwood Corp.)
OVER THE RAINBOW
(E.V. Harburg; H. Arlen; MGM
and I. Feist, Inc.)
SATURN
P.O. BOX 7124 CHICAGO, ILLINOIS 60607
772

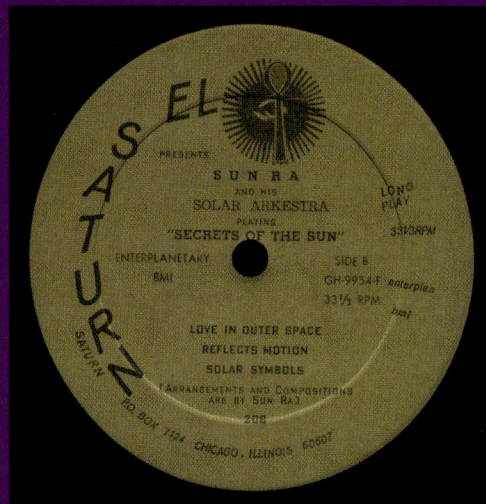

EL SATURN
PRESENTS
SUN RA
AND HIS
SOLAR ARKESTRA
PLAYING
"SECRETS OF THE SUN"
LONG PLAY
33⅓RPM
ENTERPLANETARY
BMI
SIDE B
GH-9954-F enterplan
bmi
LOVE IN OUTER SPACE
REFLECTS MOTION
SOLAR SYMBOLS
(ARRANGEMENTS AND COMPOSITIONS
ARE BY Sun Ra.)
P.O. BOX 7124 CHICAGO, ILLINOIS 60607
200

AURA SUN
℗ 1985
enterplan
bmi
ENTERPL
BMI
1. Cosmo-Party Blues
2. Space Shuttle
3. Fate in a Pleasant Mood
4. They Plan to Leave
(RA)
5626 Morton Street Philadelphia, Pa. 19144

SATURN
℗ 1979
79A
33 1/3 RPM
enterplan
bmi
SATURN
SPRINGTIME
THE DOOR OF THE COSMOS
(Compositions and Arrangements
By Sun Ra)

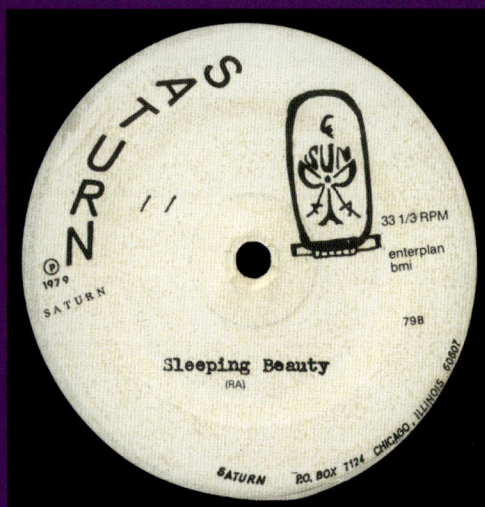

SATURN
℗ 1979
SATURN
79B
33 1/3 RPM
enterplan
bmi
Sleeping Beauty
(RA)
SATURN P.O. BOX 7124 CHICAGO, ILLINOIS 60607

EL SATURN
SUN RA
AND HIS
BLUE UNIVERSE ARKESTRA
PLAYING
"UNIVERSE IN BLUE"
LONG PLAY
33/3RPM
ESR 5000
ENTERPLAN
BMI
SIDE B
33 1/3 RPM
STEREO
enterplan
bmi
"BLACKMAN"
"IN A BLUE MOOD"
"ANOTHER SHADE OF BLUE"
(Compositions and Arrangements
are by Sun Ra.)
200
SATURN P.O. BOX 7124 CHICAGO, ILLINOIS 60607

SATURN
enterplan
bmi
80-B
THE ROSE HUE MANSIONS OF THE SUN
(Ra)
℗ 1980 Saturn

EL SATURN
SATURN
PRESENTS
THE
SUN RA ARKESTRA
LONG PLAY
33⅓RPM
SIDE B
Produced by:
Alton Abraham
VOLUME
ES752-B
enterplan
bmi
SUB UNDERGROUND SERIES
(Compositions and arrangements
are by Sun Ra.)
732
SATURN P.O. BOX 7124 CHICAGO, ILLINOIS 60607

SUN RA And His
ARKESTRA
Playing
"SOMEWHERE OVER
THE RAINBOW"

33⅓ RPM

enterplan
bmi

℗ 1977 Saturn
7877 A

WE LIVE TO BE (Ra)
GONE WITH THE WIND (Wruble)
MAKE ANOTHER MISTAKE (Ra)
TAKE THE "A" TRAIN (Strahorn)

(Compositions & Arrangements are by Sun Ra)

SATURN
5626 MORTON ST
PHILADELPHIA. PA 19144

© 1987

SIDE A

SATURN

Enterplanetary
Koncepts
BMI

RA TO THE RESCUE   chapter 1
RA TO THE RESCUE   chapter 2

FATE IN A PLEASANT MOOD

(Ra)

BMI-ENTERPLANE

7877

SIDE B

AORA

AMEN AMEN

OVER THE RAINBOW

Harburg / Arlen

I'LL WAIT FOR YOU
(Ra)

© 1977 SATURN

EL

S
A
T
U
R
N

SATURN

SUN RA
AND HIS
ARKESTRA

SIDE A

LONG
PLAY

33⅓RPM

1014077-A

© 1977

enterplan

bmi

Some Blues But Not The Kind That's Blue
(S. RA)   (Enterplan BMI)
I'll Get By   (R. Turk)   (F. Ahlert Corp.)
(ASCAP)
MY FAVORITE THINGS
(A. Hammerstein II - R. Rodgers)
(Williamson Music Corp.)

747

P.O. BOX 7124 CHICAGO, ILLINOIS 60607

I Gave Up My Death for Sun Ra   **Glenn Jones**

This happened at the jazz club Two Saints (named for its location at 2 St. Mark's Place, New York City). The Arkestra had a two-week residency at the club and I attended almost every night, driving in from my parents' house in the suburbs of northern New Jersey.

I'd first seen the Arkestra at Carnegie Hall in 1973 as part of a summer jazz series, where, at the end their set, Sun Ra, like some cosmic Pied Piper, led the group and audience out of the hall. Up West 57th Street and around the block, horn players, percussionists, singers, dancers, all dressed in glittering space-age regalia, made a joyous racket as traffic slowed to a crawl and pedestrians gawked. (John Gilmore performed a duet with an irritated truck driver who was incessantly honking his horn.) When at last they arrived at Carnegie Hall's load-in dock on West 56th, they climbed in and waved us all good night.

The second time was at Hunter College. I arrived early, grabbed a front-row seat, and saw the band in action, close up. By the end of the night I considered myself a disciple.

In 1974 the legendary jazz venue the Five Spot, which had closed in 1967, reopened as Two Saints. Soon after they booked Sun Ra and I made the 45-minute drive into the city almost every night they were there.

Over the years, I got to see Sun Ra and the various iterations of his Arkestra fifty or sixty times. For me, however, the shows at Two Saints were the most exciting. The previous gigs I'd seen had been well attended and were, to all intents, *concerts*—formal presentations of Ra's music and showcases for the band's energies and skills.

The Two Saints shows, however, were loose, sparsely attended; some nights there were more people onstage than in the audience. (The Arkestra for these shows consisted of around 15 players.) These gatherings were intimate, almost informal. Atypically, the horn players kept copies of "the band book," a five-inch-thick manila folder with lead sheets for hundreds of Sun Ra compositions and arrangements, under their seats. Over those two weeks Ra called songs I never heard the Arkestra perform before or again. He'd lean on a couple of chords or tap out a brief melodic phrase on his keyboard, the

group would grab their folders, paw frantically through until they found the piece he was signaling, then join in.

The pieces that Ra did revisit (mostly vocal numbers) were transformed show by show. One rap he returned to several times was built around the bit in *Genesis* concerning the forbidden fruit ("the tree of the knowledge of good and evil"). He varied it each time, inscrutably playing on the words "good" and "wood," as though searching himself for the parable's Greater Meaning. Finally, on the third night, he concluded with, "The tree was good. The tree was wood. The tree was woody. The tree was . . . *Woody Woodpecker*."

"They're Opening Up the Doors to the Outer Space Employment Agency" was another song he returned to several times during this period. It usually ended with Ra ambling into the audience, microphone in hand, as the band chanted behind him. Announcing that tickets were now on sale, he'd ask each of us what sort of passage we wanted for our journey, "One way or round-trip?" (I was committed—one way!)

One night Sun Ra performed "Little Sally Walker, Standing in a Saucer," though we were given to understand that the saucer Sally was standing in was *flying*. Concluding the vocal portion, Sun Ra launched into a jaw-dropping dance. Leaning out as far as he could, thrusting his arms in front of him and kicking his feet out behind, in time to the music, he appeared to be trying to levitate. Each time, as gravity did its work and it seemed certain he was about to greet terra firma with a splat, Ra would, just in time, catch himself. And then try again. And again. For a rotund man this seemed a dubious and potentially dangerous stunt, and I wasn't the only one taken aback: every member of the Arkestra appeared gobsmacked, eyes wide, mouths open, anticipating disaster.

I got to know saxophonists John Gilmore and Marshall Allen as players and to appreciate their different instrumental approaches. Sometimes Gilmore's solos would devolve down to just one or two notes, which he explored on a microscopic level, as though the whole universe might be found inside a single note. Allen, in contrast, splashed the cosmos with colors, one moment stabbing at the keys of his horn like they were too hot to touch, the next moment, cheeks puffed out, blowing lush and

Photo of Sun Ra (photographer unknown) from handmade one-off cover of *Somewhere over the Rainbow*, from collection of Glenn Jones. The fractal overlay is a trimmed patch of shower curtain, a recurring motif on hand-designed Saturn LP covers.

woozy and tender. I noted how intently the musicians listened to each other's solos; there was much mutual respect among the players.

The highlights of these shows for me were the senses-rendering explorations Ra performed nightly on his electronic keyboards. Often playing two instruments simultaneously, Ra stood with his head back, eyes fixed on something no one else could see, and let loose with a shocking barrage of thick smears, staccato beeps, roars, rumbles, and yelps, at frightening, stomach-roiling, ear-punishing levels. The thunderous, agonized beating of the low frequencies of his Moog synthesizer made the entire building quake. It felt like whole galaxies were dying and being born in those excursions. Sometimes all I could do was laugh at the outrageousness of what I was hearing; at other moments, I almost wanted to weep at what felt like heroically futile attempts to express the inexpressible. (These ventures typically lasted twenty or thirty minutes; I count them as among my happiest on Earth.)

Most shows started around 10 pm and lasted till 2 or 3 am. I was used to seeing the mighty battery of Arkestra instruments onstage when I arrived, but one night the bandstand was empty. Ten o'clock rolled around, then 11, then midnight. Finally, the door to the club opened and one of the group's percussionists dashed in, conga drum in hand, grabbing a chair as he went. Person by person, the rest of the Arkestra joined him, all at a sprint. A half hour later the entire band was onstage and in a musical frenzy.

Then Ra entered. Amid the fury, he was the quintessence of calm. With broad, flowing gestures, his cape sweeping the floor, he "conducted" the now obliterating maelstrom.

That show lasted all night. (It turned out the band had been recording that day and had rushed from the studio to the club.) When I exited, one of three or four people who'd made it through the whole night, I found myself squinting into the morning sun as the "reg'lar folk" scurried down the streets to their jobs, briefcases in hand.

One night Ra told us, "Anything can give up its life. I want you to give up your death for me." Coming to my table and grabbing a fistful of my hair, fixing my eyes with his, he implored, "Will you give up your death for me?" Holding his mic to my mouth, he awaited my answer.

How could I not?

These shows would prove to be important in another way. It was here that I got to know Richard Wilkinson, who acted as the band's road manager, film projectionist, record salesman, equipment mover—pretty much whatever needed doing, Richard was the man. After seeing me night after night, and knowing I had already snagged whatever records he was hawking, he began bringing me various stray one-offs and oddball titles he had at home. He'd pegged his customer!

Three years later I was living in Somerville, Massachusetts, working for the indie distribution arm of Rounder Records. We carried a few hundred of the leading folk, jazz, blues, and world music labels of the time. A dozen or so people labored there, in a windowless cinderblock warehouse about the size of a six-car garage. The floors were concrete slabs, dank and cracked; the toilet leaked, leaving a little stream that meandered through the warehouse and froze in the winter. There was a single heater for the whole building—a fan mounted in a wobbly metal box on the ceiling, which, when it snapped on, blew papers and packing peanuts into the air like snow. In the coldest New England months, we worked in hats and gloves.

All for $2.10 an hour and all the crud we could inhale. But no one could have convinced us that we weren't the luckiest people in the world: we got to work around *music*.

Early in my tenure, I recommended that we add Saturn to our catalog of labels. I did my best to convince the powers that be that there was great demand for these records, and that since the only way you could obtain them was to buy them from the band at shows, we would be the sole distributor of the label. (I confess that one reason for pushing this agenda was to gain an inside track to records that were otherwise impossible for *me* to find.)

A couple of our salesmen were jazz heads (including Richard Seidel, who would make his name after leaving Rounder) who supported my suggestion. I was given the go-ahead to negotiate terms with the label. I called the Ra house on Morton Street in Philadelphia and was told to see Danny Thompson, the Arkestra's baritone saxophonist and flautist, at his grocery store, Pharaoh's Den, in Philly's Germantown district.

A few weeks later I pulled up in front of the place. The sign over the door displayed a painting of Pharaoh (who resembled Sun Ra) and the legend "Pharaoh feed [sic] the nations of the world for seven years." Inside were racks of Tastykake pastries (a Germantown institution), a couple of pinball machines, some homemade Sun Ra hats, and a few copies of the group's latest LP.

I remember Danny, in his red-tinted glasses, chatting coolly with me while ticking off the kids who'd stopped by the store on their way home from school, seemingly just to harass the poor guy.

Finally, jotting down my phone number, he said, "OK, someone will be in touch." I'd hoped to visit the band at the Morton Street house, but that wasn't to be. I drove back to Boston.

The next call I received was from Richard Wilkinson. He invited me to meet with him and Sun Ra in New York City "to discuss terms." We agreed on a date—sometime in December 1977—and a location—a restaurant on 42nd Street that Sun Ra especially liked.

I met Richard at the eatery, but he was alone. Sun Ra had decided to see *Close Encounters of the Third Kind,* which had premiered a month earlier and was now playing at a giant multiplex somewhere in the East 50s.

The scene at the multiplex was chaos—snaking, block-long queues waited to buy tickets to one of dozens of theaters screening the film round the clock. Announcements came buzzing over bullhorns; police rode around the square on horseback, squeezing through the milling crowds, blowing whistles, attempting to maintain order. Even someone as singular as Sun Ra was impossible to find in such a massive throng. After skirting the crowd in vain, Richard and I made our way back to the restaurant.

Wilkinson and I continued this back-and-forth for six hours. It was getting dark when, finally, we ran into Sun Ra on the street. Wearing headphones with big square earpieces, the headphone cord dragging along on the sidewalk behind him, he was eating an orange and nonchalantly tossing bits of peel into the gutter.

We were in front of a Burger King, and Sun Ra suggested we have our meeting inside. For the next few delirious hours, Ra did all the talking. There was some discussion of *Close Encounters* and how John Williams had stolen Sun Ra's music for the soundtrack, including the main four-note theme; of politics, especially race politics, and how respectfully black artists were treated overseas versus how poorly they were treated in the U.S.; of the Bible, and how, although true, it represented "a

bad truth," and how Ra viewed his job, as *A* creator, to impress *THE* Creator, to astonish Him so much that He'd alter the ugly truths of scriptural prophecy and create a world of joy in place of the dark one we were forced to suffer in. He even told a few racist jokes, on blacks and on whites.

At the end of all this, Sun Ra asked, "So, what is your proposition?" Anything I could have said at that moment would have felt so mundane—so Earthly—that I was speechless. Eventually I managed to mumble something like, "Well, we'll pay you $2.65 per record; stores will buy them from us for $3.75, and sell them for $5.95."

In spite of my fumbling, I'd passed whatever test I'd been given. Thus began one of the stranger relationships I had in my twenty-three years in the music biz. Typically, Danny Thompson would call, raving about the new records, hot off the press, the likes of which, he assured me, no one had ever heard before. ("This is what *Disco* is going to sound like in the year *3000*!!") I'd order 200 copies, and a day or two later he'd fly to Boston's Logan Airport with boxes of records; I'd meet

ROUNDUP RECORDS 1982 CATALOG

You Are Not Alone

Your Alternative Music Source!

16

__424 George Freeman *Birth Sign*
__425 Kalaparusha Maurice McIntyre *Forces & Feelings*
__426 Sonny Stitt *Made For Each Other*
__427 Jimmy Forrest/Elvin Jones/Grant Green
__428 Joseph Jarman & Anthony Braxton *Together Alone*
__429 Tab Smith *Because of You*
__430 Muhal Richard Abrams *Things to Come From Those Now Gone*
__431 Paul Bascomb *Bad Bascomb*
__432/433 Art Ensemble of Chicago *Live At Mandel Hall* (2 LP)
__434 Chris Woods *Somebody Done Stole My Blues*
__435 Jimmy Forrest *Night Train*
__436 Frank Walton *Intensity* with Henry Threadgill
__437 Chris Woods *Modus Operandi*
__603 *The Legend of Sleepy John Estes*
__605 Curtis Jones *Lonesome Bedroom Blues*
__606 Yank Rachell *Mandolin Blues*
__607 Roosevelt Sykes *Hard Drivin' Blues*
__608 Sleepy John Estes *Broke & Hungry*
__613 Sleepy John Estes *Brownsville Blues*
__614 Arthur "Big Boy" Crudup *Look On Yonder's Wall*
__616 Roosevelt Sykes *in Europe*
__617 J.B. Hutto *Hawk Squat!*
__619 Sleepy John Estes (w/Earl Hooker, Carey Bell, Jimmy Dawkins) *Electric Sleep*
__620 Magic Sam *Black Magic*
__622 Carey Bell *Blues Harp*
__623 Jimmy Dawkins *Fast Fingers*
__624 *Chicago Ain't Nothin' But a Blues Band*
__625 Luther Allison *Love Me Mama*
__627 Big Joe Williams *9 String Guitar*
__628 Junior Wells *South Side Blues Jam*
__629 Mighty Joe Young *Touch of Soul*
__631 Eddie Vinson *Old Kidney Stew Is Fine* with Jay McShann, T-Bone Walker
__632 Roosevelt Sykes *Feel Like Blowin'*
__633 T-Bone Walker *I Want a Little Girl*
__635 Junior Wells *On Tap*
__636 J.B. Hutto & the Hawks *Slidewinder*
__637 Edith Wilson *He May Be Your Man But He Comes to See Me Sometimes*
__638 Otis Rush *Cold Day in Hell*
__640 Junior Wells *Blues Hit Big Town*
__641 Jimmy Dawkins *Blisterstring*
__643 Otis Rush *So Many Roads*
__644 Jimmy Johnson *Johnson's Whacks*

DELUXE

__601 Fats Waller *Fine Arabian Stuff*
__602 Earl Hines *The Legendary Little Theatre Concert of 1964, Vol. 1*

DINGLE'S (import)

__301 *Dingle's Regatta*
__302 Packie Byrne and Bonnie Shaljean *The Half Door*
__303 Jim Mageean *The Capstan Bar*
__304 Fiddler's Dream *To See The Play*
__305 Ar Log (Welsh folk group)
__306 Nick Dow *Burd Margaret*
__307 Sam Stephens & Annie Lennox *The Pretty Ploughboy*
__308 Graham and Eileen Pratt *To Friend and Foe*
__309 Oyster Ceilidh Band *Jack's Alive*
__310 *Ar Log II*
__311 Packie Byrne & Bonnie Shaljean *Rountower*
__312 Pyewackett
__314 Jake Thackray *And Songs*
__711 Fiddler's Dram

DIRTY SHAME

__1238 Daryl Ott *River Front Rags & Blues*
__1239 Ben Conroy & Charlie Booty *Barrelhouse Boogie*
__2002 New Black Eagle Jazz Band *On the River*
√2003 Waldo's Gutbucket Syncopaters *Harlem Jazz Hot Style*
__4553 Steve Hancoff *Classic Ragtime Guitar*

EARWIG

__4901 The Jelly Roll Kings *Rockin' The Juke Joint Down*

EAT

__ONE The Commercials *Compare and Decide*

EL SATURN
Not all El Saturn records are always in stock. Here is a complete listing; please reorder if titles you want are not immediately available.

__CMIJ78 Sun Ra *Disco 3000*
__165 Sun Ra *with Pharaoh Sanders*
__200 Sun Ra *Universe in Blue*
__203 Sun Ra *Interstellar Low Ways*
__216 Sun Ra *Super Sonic Sounds*
__406 Sun Ra *Nubians of Plutonia*
__407 Sun Ra *Angels and Demons*
__408 Sun Ra *Cosmic Tunes for Mental Therapy*
__409 Sun Ra *We Travel The Spaceways*
__485 Sun Ra *Deep Purple*
__502 Sun Ra *Strange Strings*
__507 Sun Ra *Atlantis*
__508 Sun Ra *Holiday for Soul Dance*
__509 Sun Ra *Mondrails and Satellites*
__512 Sun Ra *Sound Sun Pleasure*
__519 Sun Ra *Mondrails & Satellites, Vol. 2*
__520 Sun Ra *Continuation*
__521 Sun Ra *My Brother the Wind, Vol. 1*
__522 Sun Ra *Night of the Purple Moon*
__524 Lacy Gibson *I Wish I Had A Wishing Ring*
__532 Sun Ra *Bad & Beautiful*
__538 Sun Ra *Discipline 27*
__711 Sun Ra *Magic City*
__771 Sun Ra *Soul Vibration of Man*
__772 Sun Ra *Taking A Chance on Chances*
__1272 Sun Ra *Live in Egypt, Vol. 1*
__1981 Sun Ra & his Arkestra
__5221 Sun Ra *Brother the Wind, Vol. 2*
__6680 Sun Ra *I, Pharaoh*
__7877 Sun Ra *Somewhere Over the Rainbow*
__9954 Sun Ra *Secrets of the Sun*
__9956 Sun Ra *Angels & Demons at Play*
__10480 Sun Ra *Aurora Borealis*
__11179 Sun Ra and his Arkestra *Sleeping Beauty*
__14200 Sun Ra *Space Probe*
__19782 Sun Ra & the Arkestra *Sound Mirror*
__19783 Sun Ra & the Arkestra *Media Dream*
__52375 Sun Ra *What's New*
__61674 Sun Ra *Discipline 99*
__72579 Sun Ra and his Arkestra *God Is More Than Love Could Ever Be*
__77771 Sun Ra *Nidhamu*
__81774 Sun Ra *The Antique Blacks*
__91379 Sun Ra and his Arkestra *Omniverse*
__91780 Sun Ra
__92074 Sun Ra *Sub Underground*
__98766 Sun Ra *Other Planes of There*
__99561 Sun Ra *Art Forms of Dimensions Tomorrow*
__99562 Sun Ra *Fate In A Pleasant Mood*
__101679 Sun Ra and his Arkestra *On Jupiter*
__144000 Sun Ra *The Invisible Shield*
__995611 Sun Ra *Visits Planet Earth*
__1014077 Sun Ra *My Favorite Things*
__1217718 Sun Ra *Horizon*

EMBER

(See Relic)

EMILY

__9578 Anita O'Day *Live in Tokyo*
__11279 Anita O'Day *My Ship*
__11579 Anita O'Day *Live At Mingo's*
__13081 Anita O'Day *Angel Eyes*
√102479 Anita O'Day *Live At The City*

ESCA

__1300 John Lincoln Wright *Takin' Old Route 1*

ETIQUETTE

__26 The Wallers *Out of Our Tree*

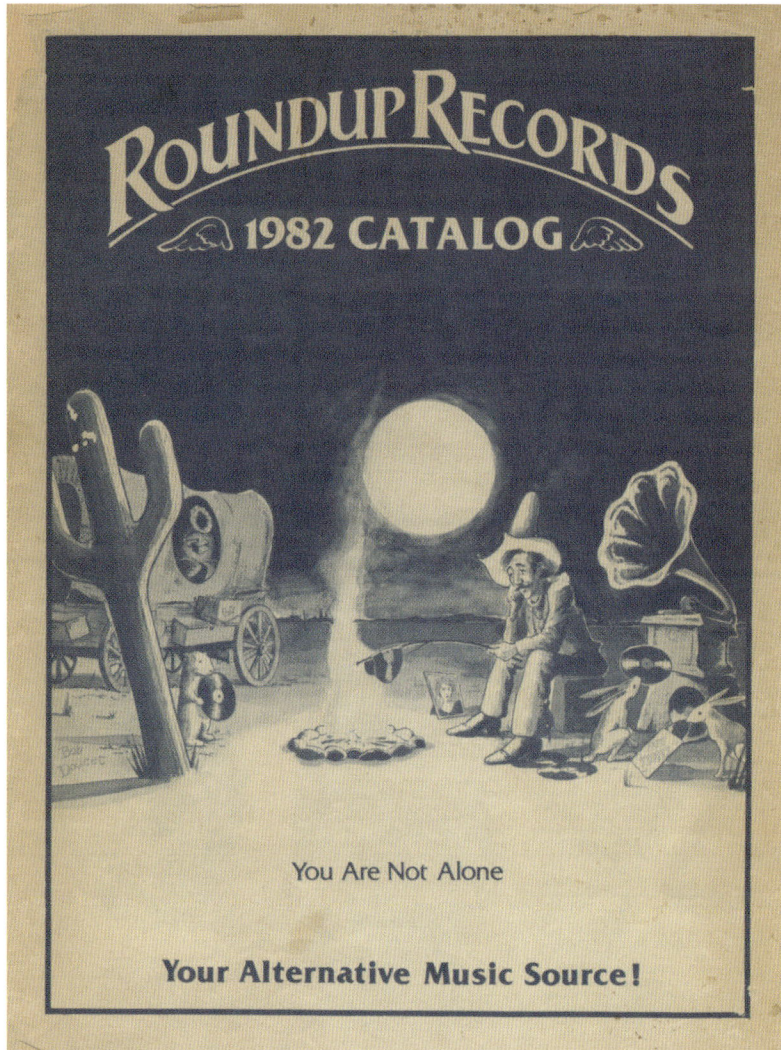

Rounder Records (the label) had a wholesale arm, Rounder Distribution, which distributed its own releases as well as those of 200 or so independent labels. Rounder also had a retail mail-order division called Roundup. Each division issued its own catalog (collection Bill Morrison).

---

him at the baggage carousel, hand over a thick envelope of cash (*always*), and Danny would catch the next plane back to Philly.

By the late '70s, the Arkestra was getting more frequent overseas bookings. Their LP sales to Rounder, I later learned, helped pay for passports, visas, and travel expenses. Whenever the band needed money (*always*), Sun Ra would select the recordings, send them out to be pressed, and Danny would call me. Over the years, we carried maybe sixty different Saturn LPs, several 45s, cassettes, and copies of Ra's poetry book, *The Immeasurable Equation*.

Distributing Saturn product posed a number of problems. The records had no catalog numbers, many weren't titled, and they were delivered without shrinkwrap. To distribute the records to stores, we needed to provide these details.

With the latest LP in hand, I'd type out album and song titles and assign each record a catalog number (typically, the matrix number engraved in the record's lead-off grooves). When I wasn't sure of an album's title, I'd call Danny or Sun Ra for confirmation. (There were, however, instances when I phoned to find that the band was already on their way overseas. With no one to verify an album title, I named it myself, usually based on what seemed to be the album's main track, e.g., *Rose Hue Mansions of the Sun*. I see now that besides sowing confusion for future discographers, this was hubris writ large. I hereby apologize.)

I photocopied the info sheets on colored paper and taped them to the back covers (*see right*); then we had the records shrinkwrapped. In the decades since, I've seen these records all over the world, in stores, in people's collections, for auction online. If that info sheet is still taped to the back cover, the record at one time passed through my hands. (An accomplishment that, along with six bucks, gets me a large coffee at Starbucks.)

Once I'd shuttled those LPs from the airport back to our fusty warehouse, one of life's joys was breaking open the boxes and reveling in the covers—an exciting event in which everyone partook. It was like Christmas! The top ten or twenty albums in each box were elaborately hand-decorated; some were colored with markers; others were embellished, collage style, with bits of metallic paper and snapshots; the so-called shower curtain covers featured 8 × 10 glossy photos sealed under sheets of clear patterned plastic. (One of mine preserves an anonymous member of the Arkestra's beard hair.) As we dug deeper into the boxes, the covers got less interesting, some having only a perfunctory Magic Marker scrawl across a generic sleeve.

I typically ordered 200 copies of each new release. Though I tried to reorder additional copies as the records sold out (*always*), none—so far as I know—was ever re-pressed. The band may have hung on to a few copies to sell at shows, and they sold some directly to Third Street Jazz in Philly, but it seems that they pressed but a few hundred copies of each title, most of which we bought and sent out into the world.

Eventually Alton Abraham, who ran the Chicago branch of Saturn, called. This led to our carrying some Saturn back catalog he still had in stock, most from the '60s and early '70s—albums with "real" (mass-printed) covers. It took forever to get stock from Alton; he sometimes assured me he had hundreds of copies of a back title, but he could find and ship only a few. This was frustrating, especially as we paid in advance, but Alton was ever the gentleman, cautioning me to thank the Creator and not to eat too much.

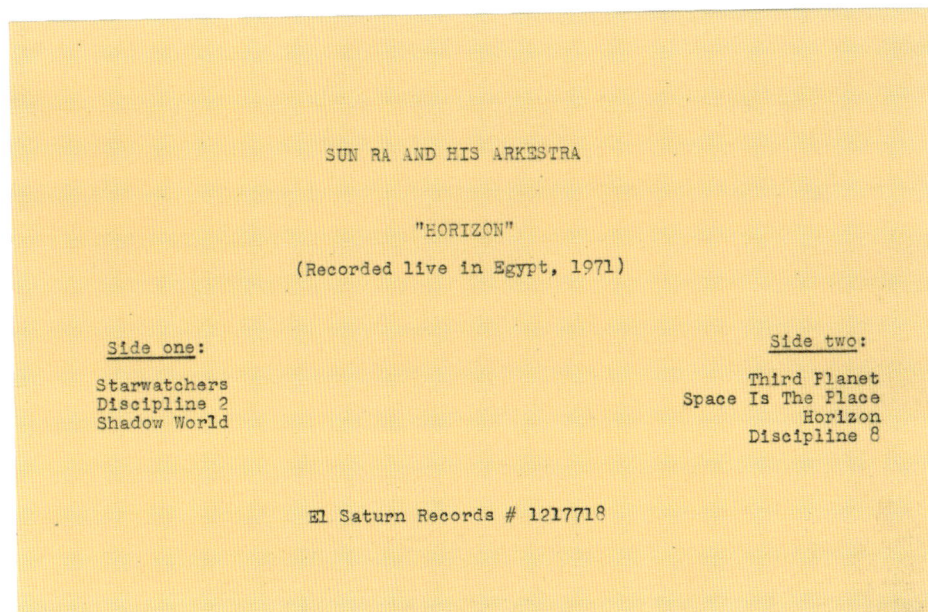

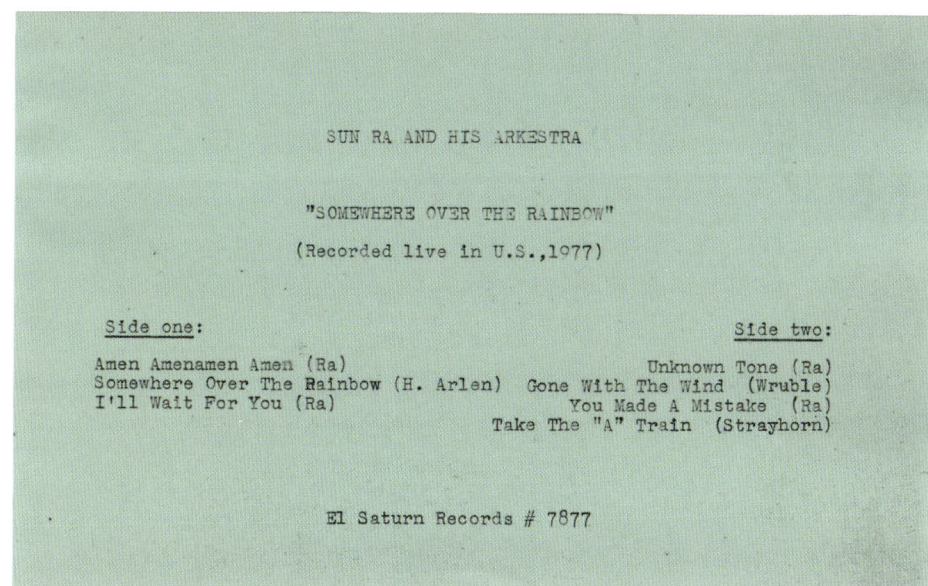

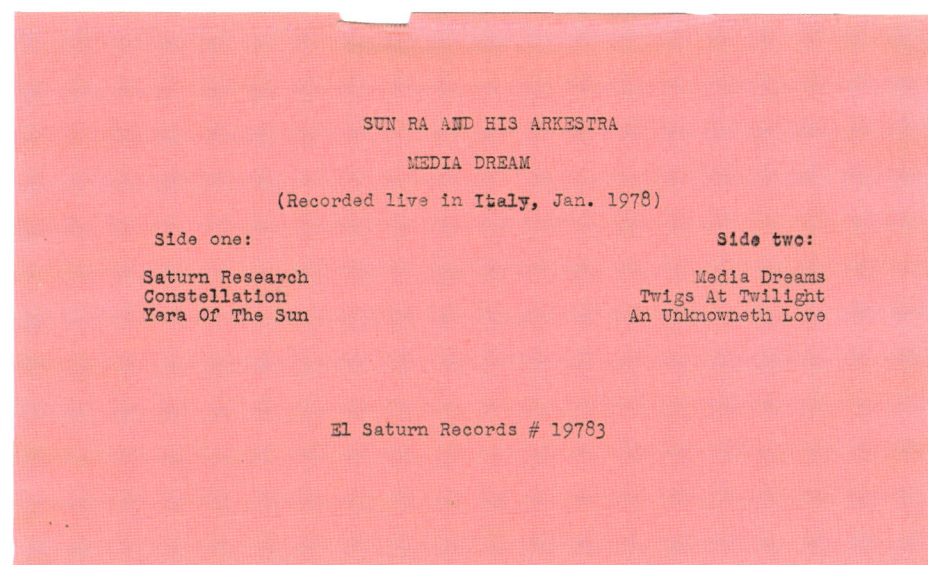

SUN RA AND HIS ARKESTRA

"HORIZON"

(Recorded live in Egypt, 1971)

Side one:

Starwatchers
Discipline 2
Shadow World

Side two:

Third Planet
Space Is The Place
Horizon
Discipline 8

El Saturn Records # 1217718

SUN RA AND HIS ARKESTRA

"SOMEWHERE OVER THE RAINBOW"

(Recorded live in U.S.,1977)

Side one:

Amen Amenamen Amen (Ra)
Somewhere Over The Rainbow (H. Arlen)
I'll Wait For You (Ra)

Side two:

Unknown Tone (Ra)
Gone With The Wind (Wruble)
You Made A Mistake (Ra)
Take The "A" Train (Strayhorn)

El Saturn Records # 7877

SUN RA AND HIS ARKESTRA

MEDIA DREAM

(Recorded live in Italy, Jan. 1978)

Side one:

Saturn Research
Constellation
Yera Of The Sun

Side two:

Media Dreams
Twigs At Twilight
An Unknowneth Love

El Saturn Records # 19783

I continued to cross paths with Ra. A few weeks before a series of shows at the newly restored Modern Theater in downtown Boston, in December 1978, Ra came to the city by bus. I picked him up at the Trailways station and chauffeured him to the loft of Bill Sebastian, a young genius who had built what he called his "Outerspace Visual Communicator." The OVC was an immense projection-screen-cum-light-show, consisting of dozens of self-contained Plexiglas cells arrayed into a hexagonal, beehive-like structure. Each cell was several feet deep, with hundreds of wires coming out the back, each capable of producing every color in the spectrum, in every possible intensity, from barely discernible to eyeball melting. This elaborate machine was controlled by a touch-sensitive keypad, a miniature version of the screen itself, mounted on a console.

Bill had spent several years constructing the OVC while listening to Sun Ra records almost exclusively. Having witnessed Sebastian's invention, Sun Ra invited him to join the group onstage for their twelve-day stint at the Modern. This series of concerts almost rivaled the Two Saints shows of four years earlier.

In 1979 Rounder Records signed Sun Ra to a three-album deal. I went down to NYC and got to be a fly on the wall for the sessions for the first album, *Strange Celestial Road* (released in 1980).

Over the years, I made a point to see every Sun Ra show within striking distance of Boston. They were always enjoyable, and many were remarkable. The last time I saw Sun Ra perform was at Nightstage in Cambridge, in 1991. Having suffered a series of strokes, he was in a wheelchair and had to be hoisted onstage, but he played as splendidly as ever.

Looking back on all this, I consider myself very lucky. How gratifying it was to have walked the Earth at the same time as Sun Ra, and to have been—peripherally, briefly—a part of his orbit, and part of the mechanism that delivered his extraordinary music to the world.

And I'm pleased to say that, to date, I've kept the promise I made to the man in 1974.

Postscript: Two days after I finished writing this reminiscence in March 2020, Danny Ray Thompson, who played such a key role in this story, died. These notes are dedicated to his memory.

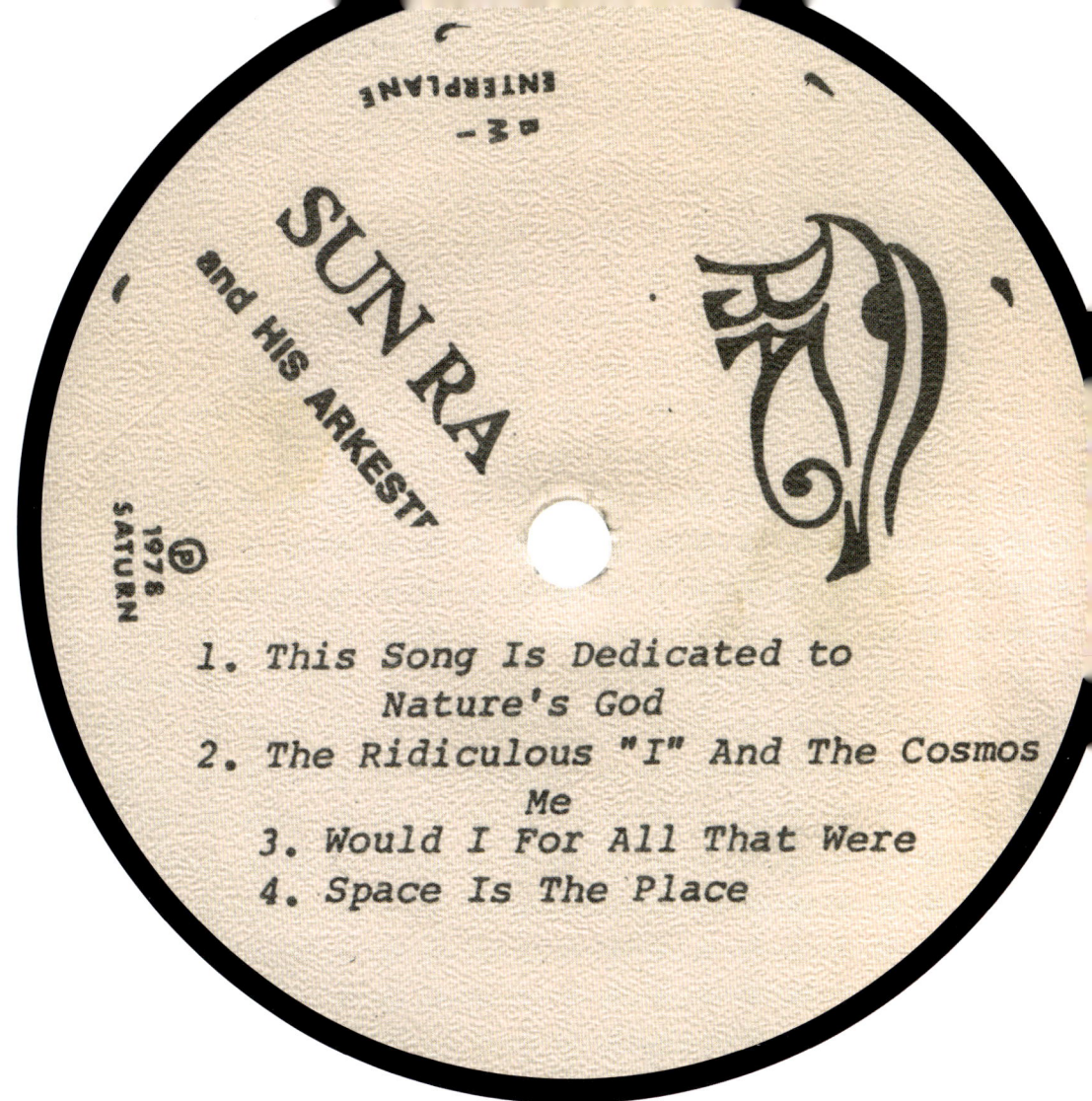

Glenn Jones's extensive record collection began with the purchase of Soupy Sales's "Do the Mouse" (with pic sleeve) in 1965. In 1977 Jones was hired as a buyer for the distribution arm of Rounder Records, for which he signed dozens of labels, among them Sun Ra's Saturn. Jones has produced and/or written liner notes for many records, mostly by American primitive guitarists John Fahey and Robbie Basho, and assembled the genre's premier anthology, *The Thousand Incarnations of the Rose*, for Craft Records. For 19 years Jones led the instrumental rock band Cul de Sac, which recorded nine albums, including collaborations with Fahey and Can's Damo Suzuki. In 2004 he issued the first of several solo acoustic guitar albums. Jones lives in Cambridge with his wife, Nora, their cat, Hopscotch, some 10,000 LPs, and mountains of guitars and banjos.

SATURN HANDMADE COVERS

Rachmaninoff

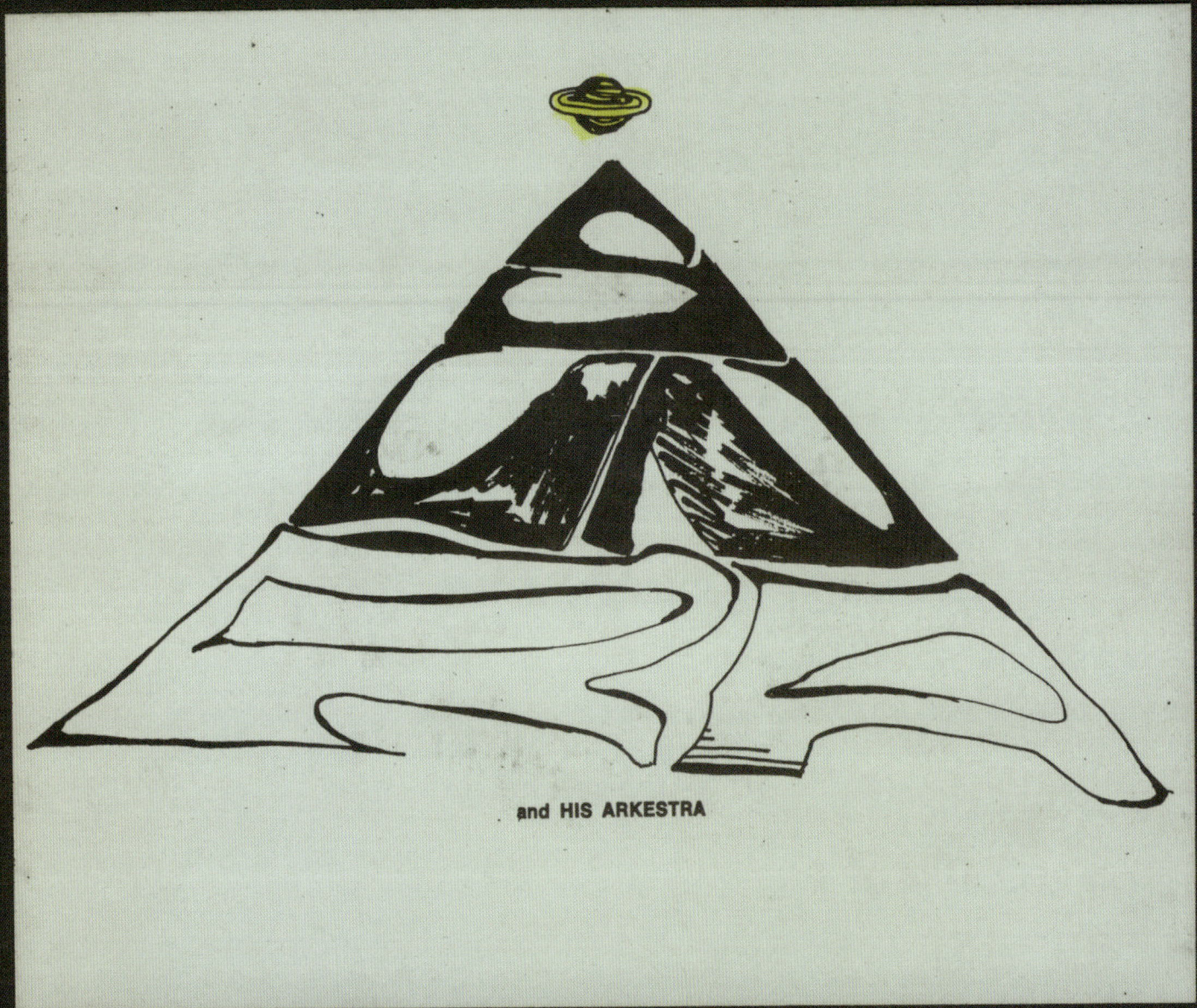

and HIS ARKESTRA

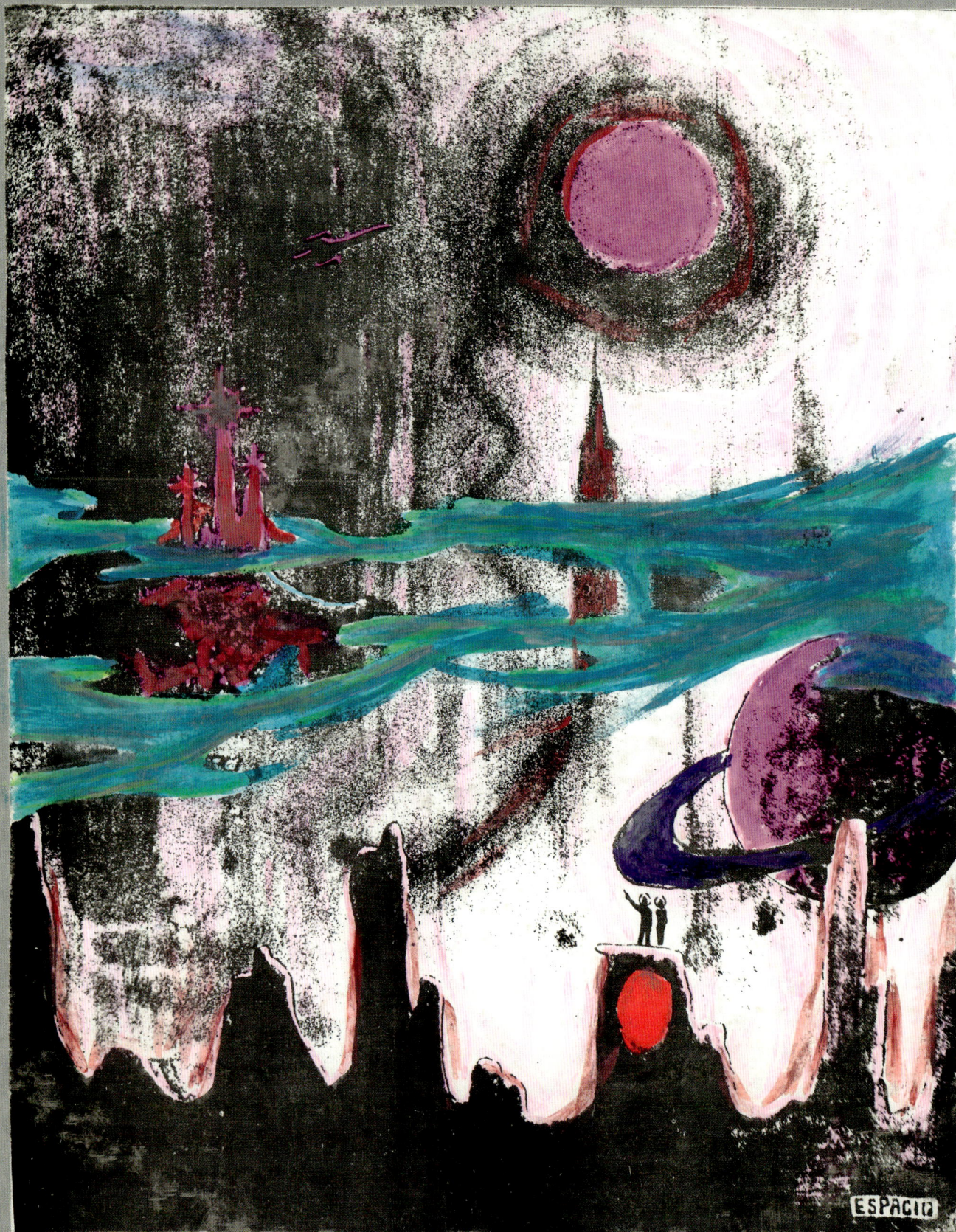

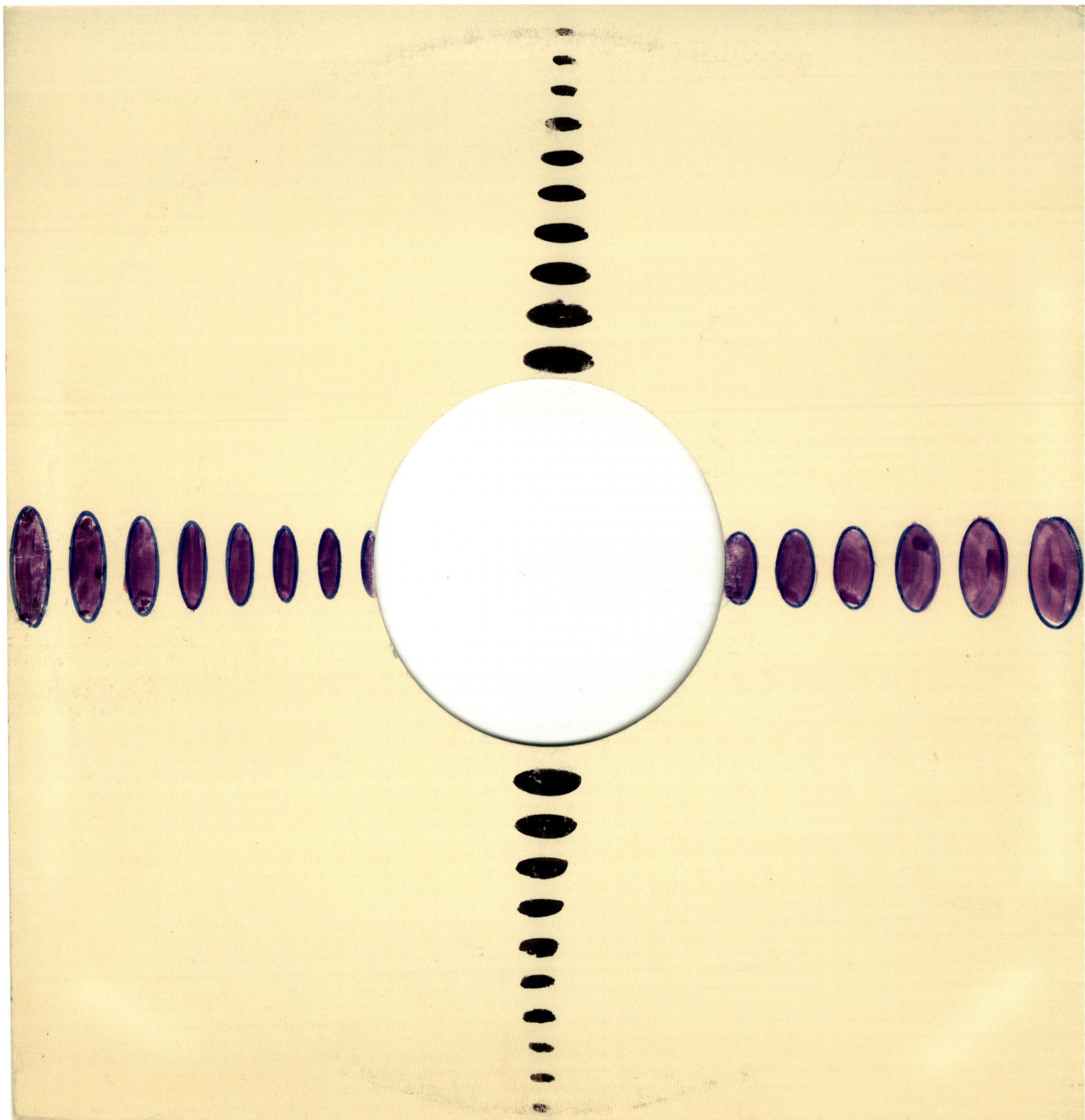

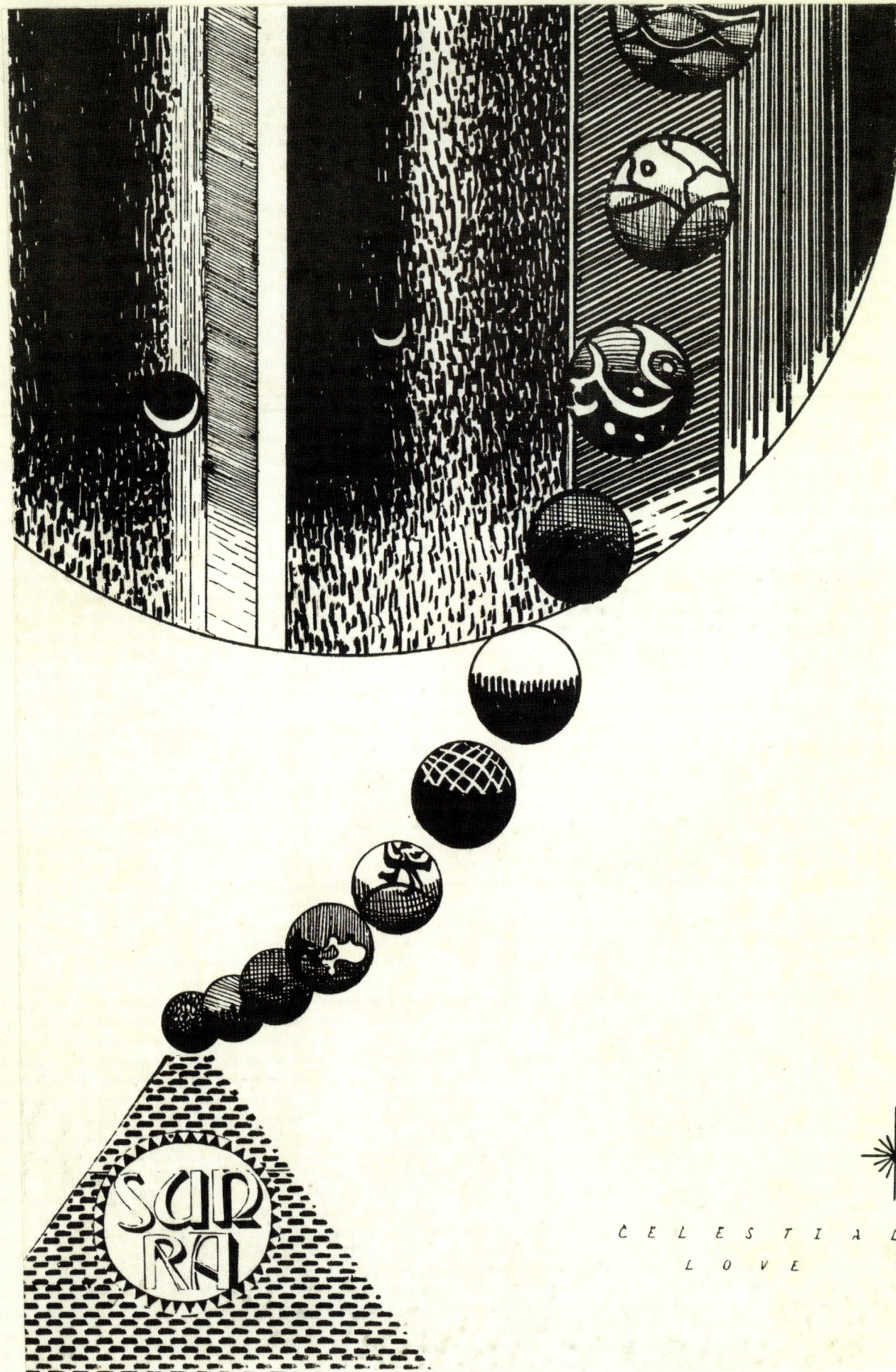

CELESTIAL
LOVE

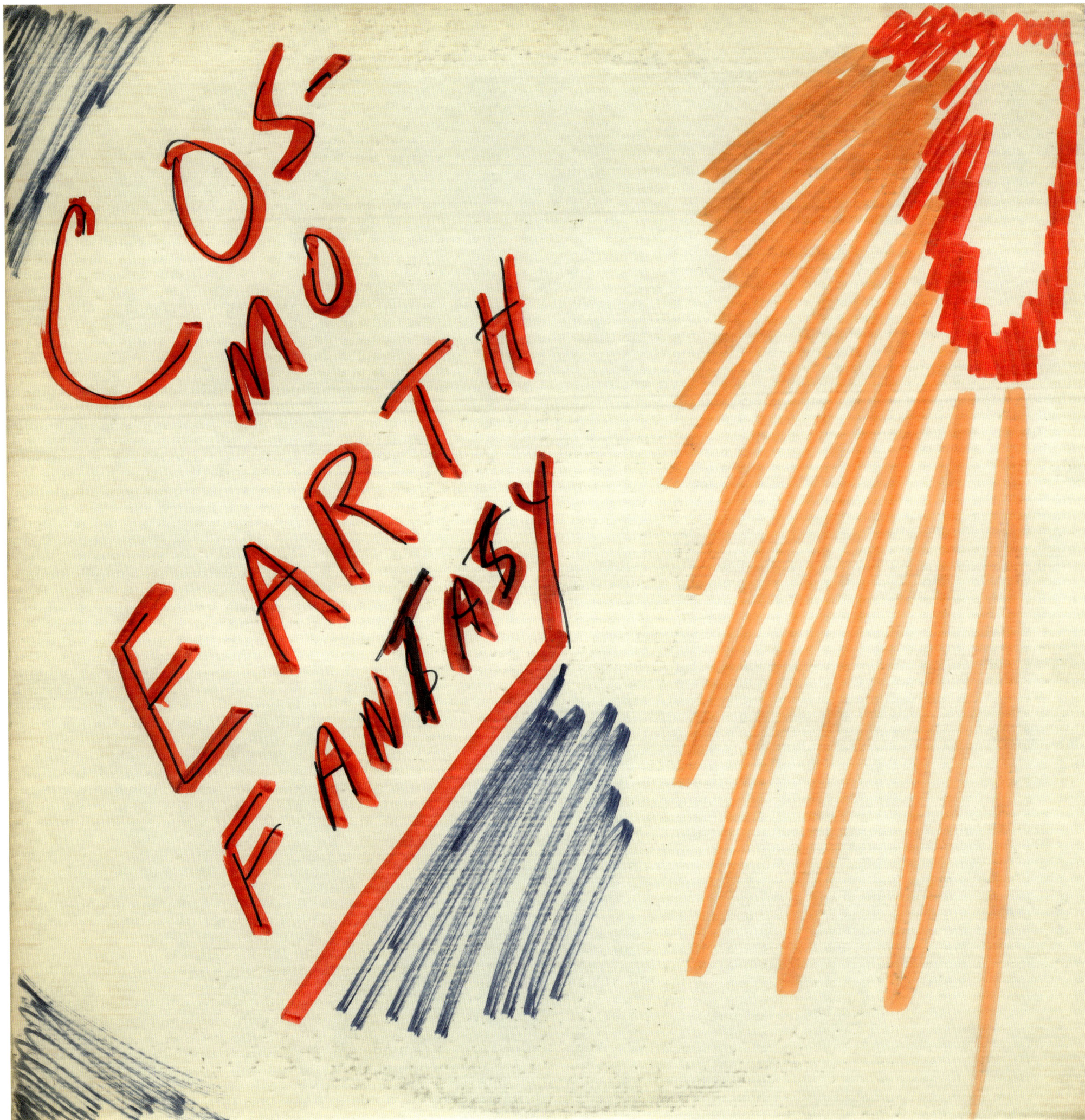

COSMO
EARTH
FANTASY

COSMO EARTH FANTASY

COSMO-EARTH
FANTASY

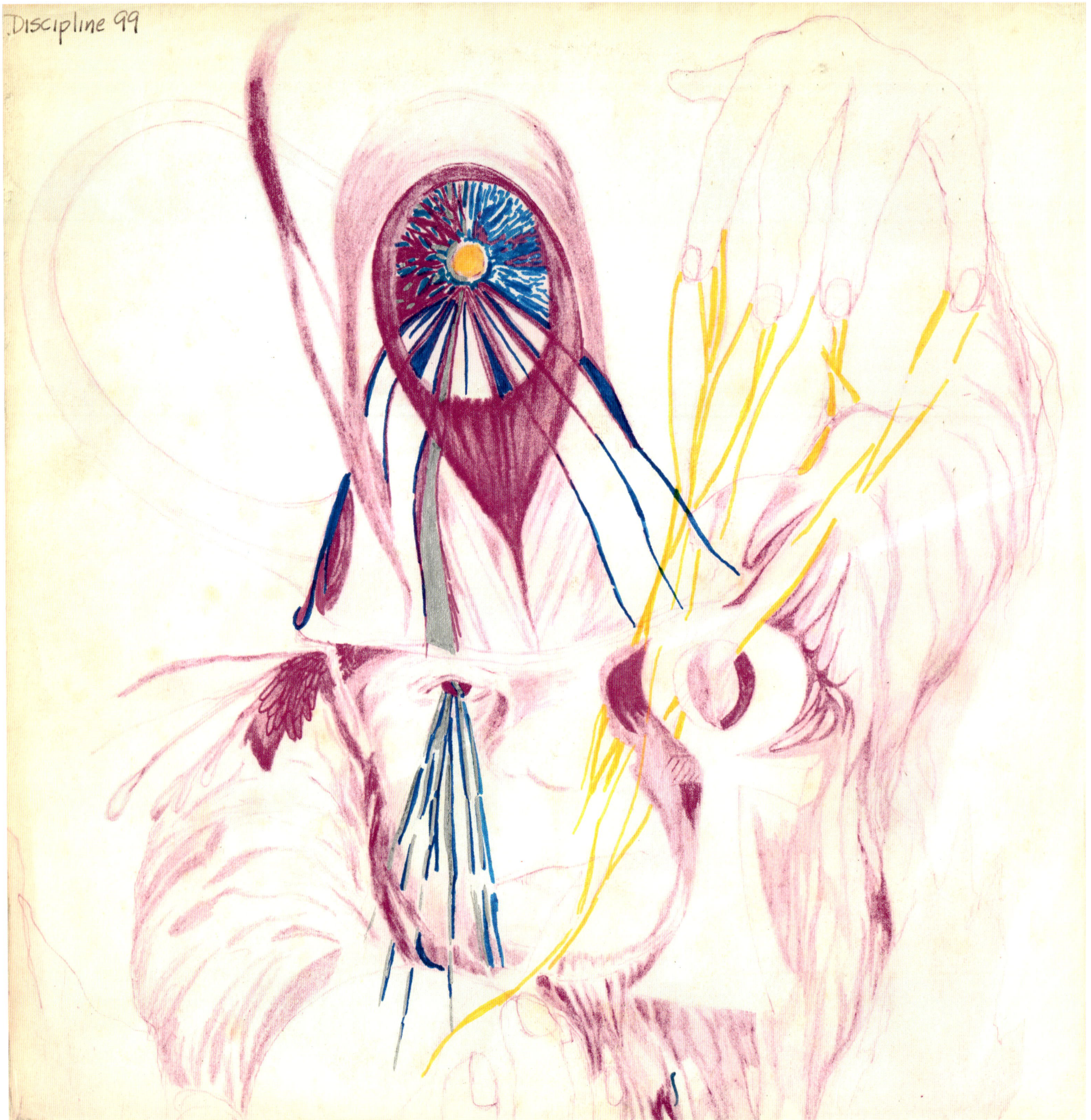

DISCO 3000

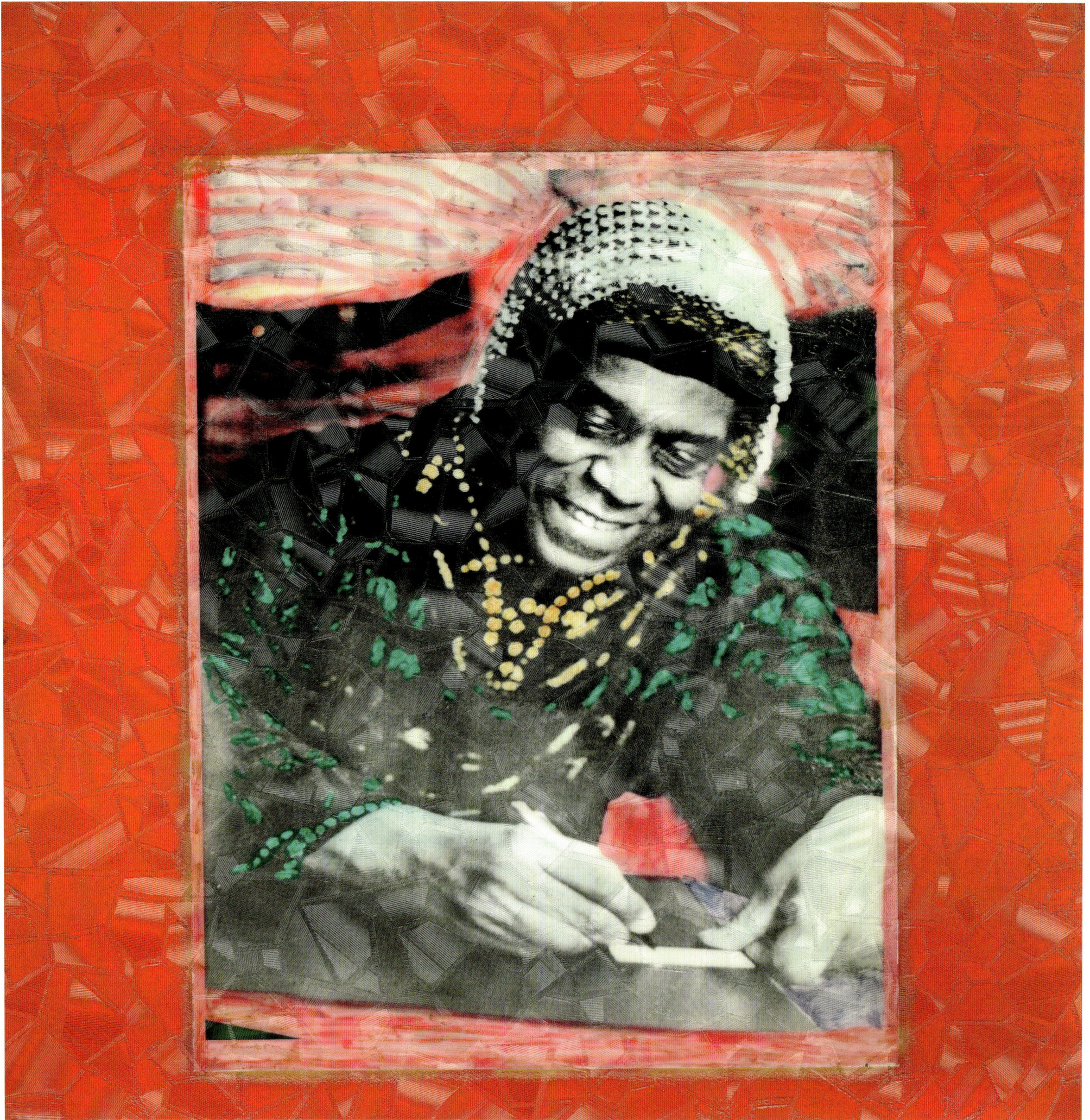

God is More Than Love Can Ever Be

SunRA Days of Happiness

Saturn 72579

405 579 11
ACADEMY PRICE
$ 60.00

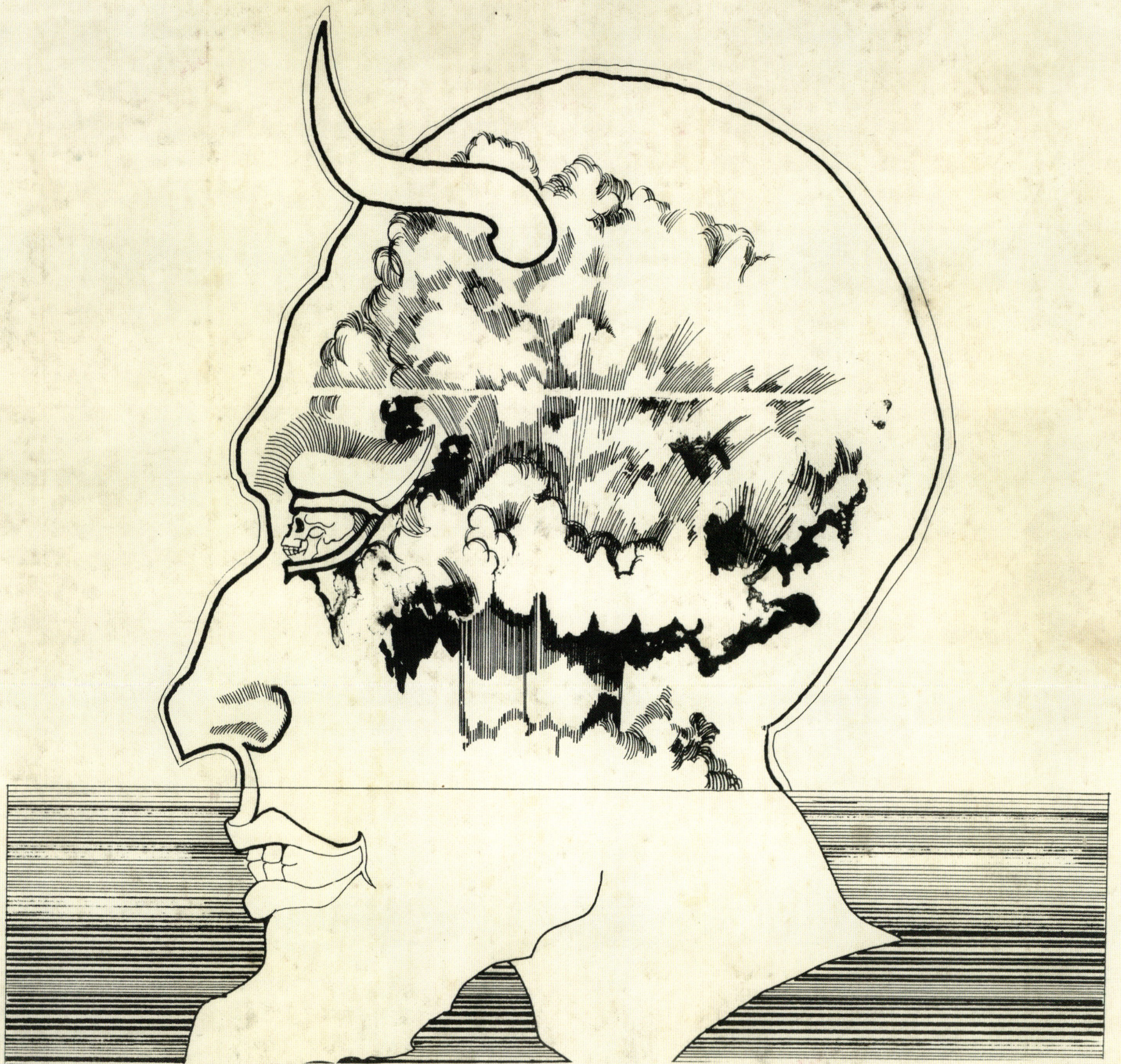

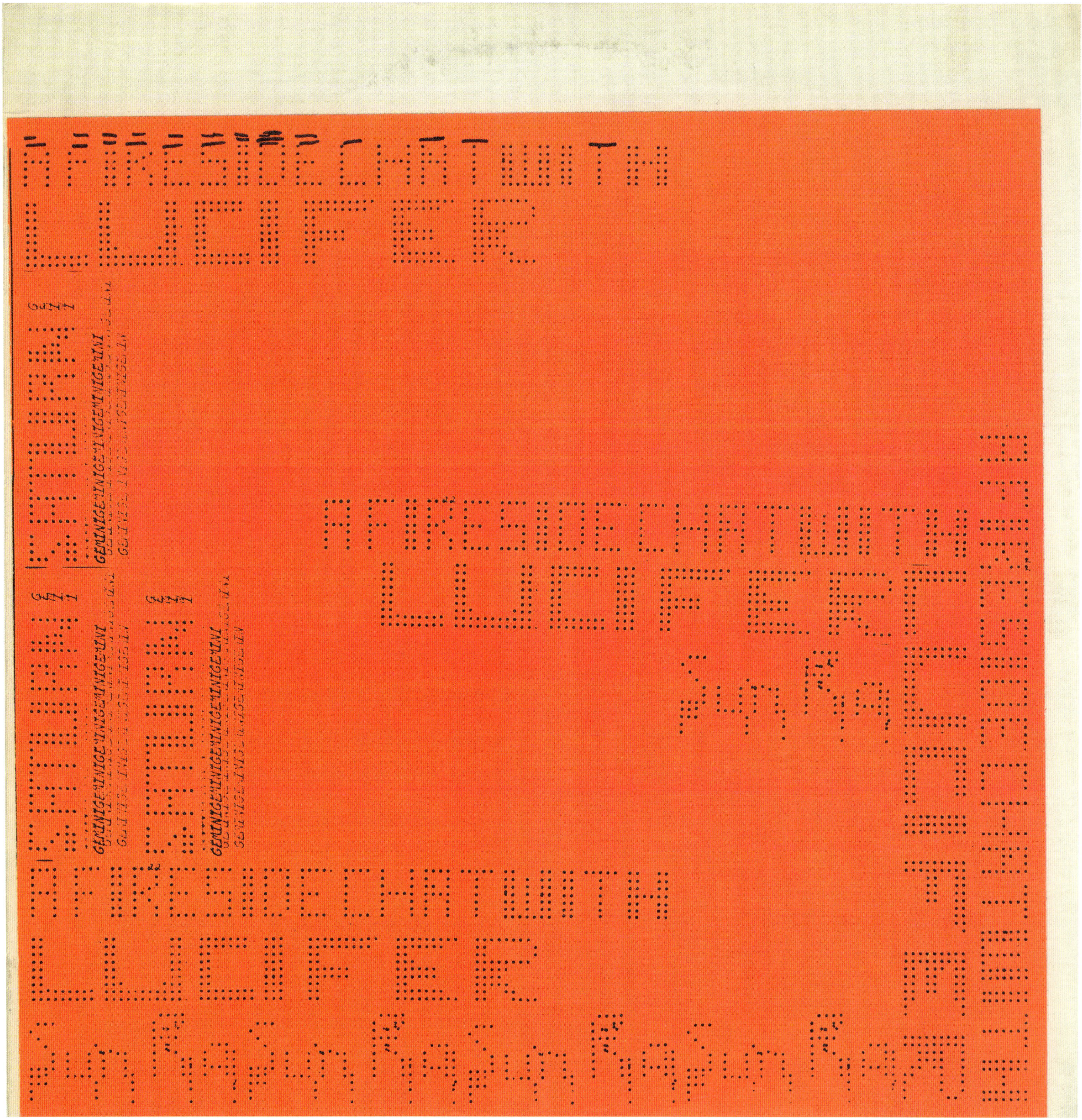

A FIRESIDE CHAT WITH
LUCIFER
Sun Ra

A FIRESIDE CHAT WITH
LUCIFER

A FIRESIDE CHAT WITH

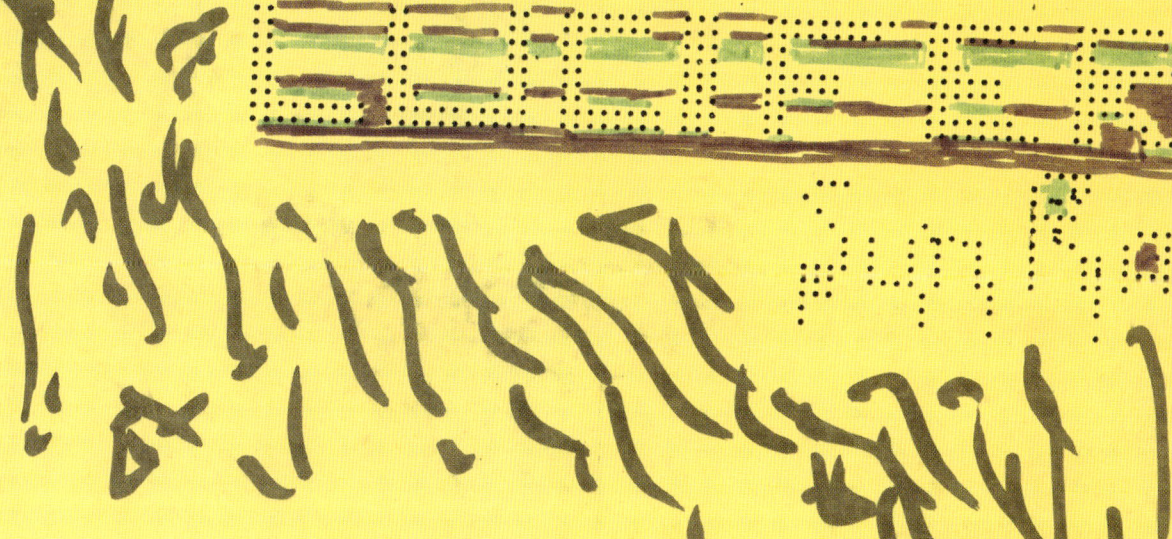

A FIRESIDE CHAT WITH

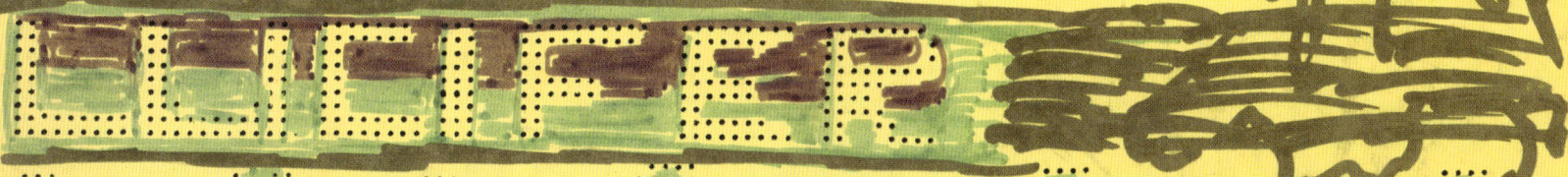

A FIRESIDE CHAT WITH LUCIFER

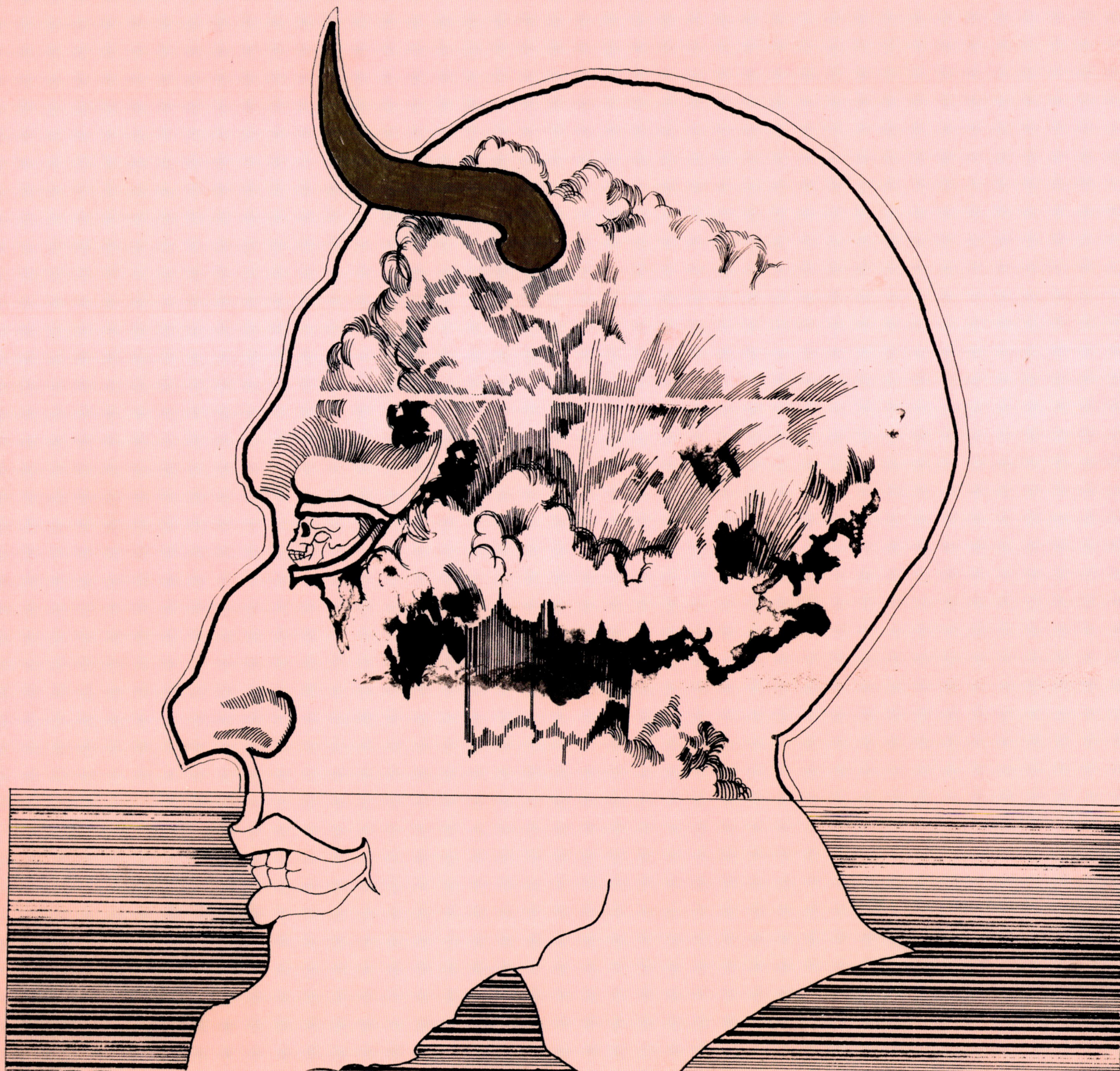

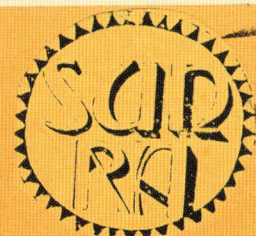

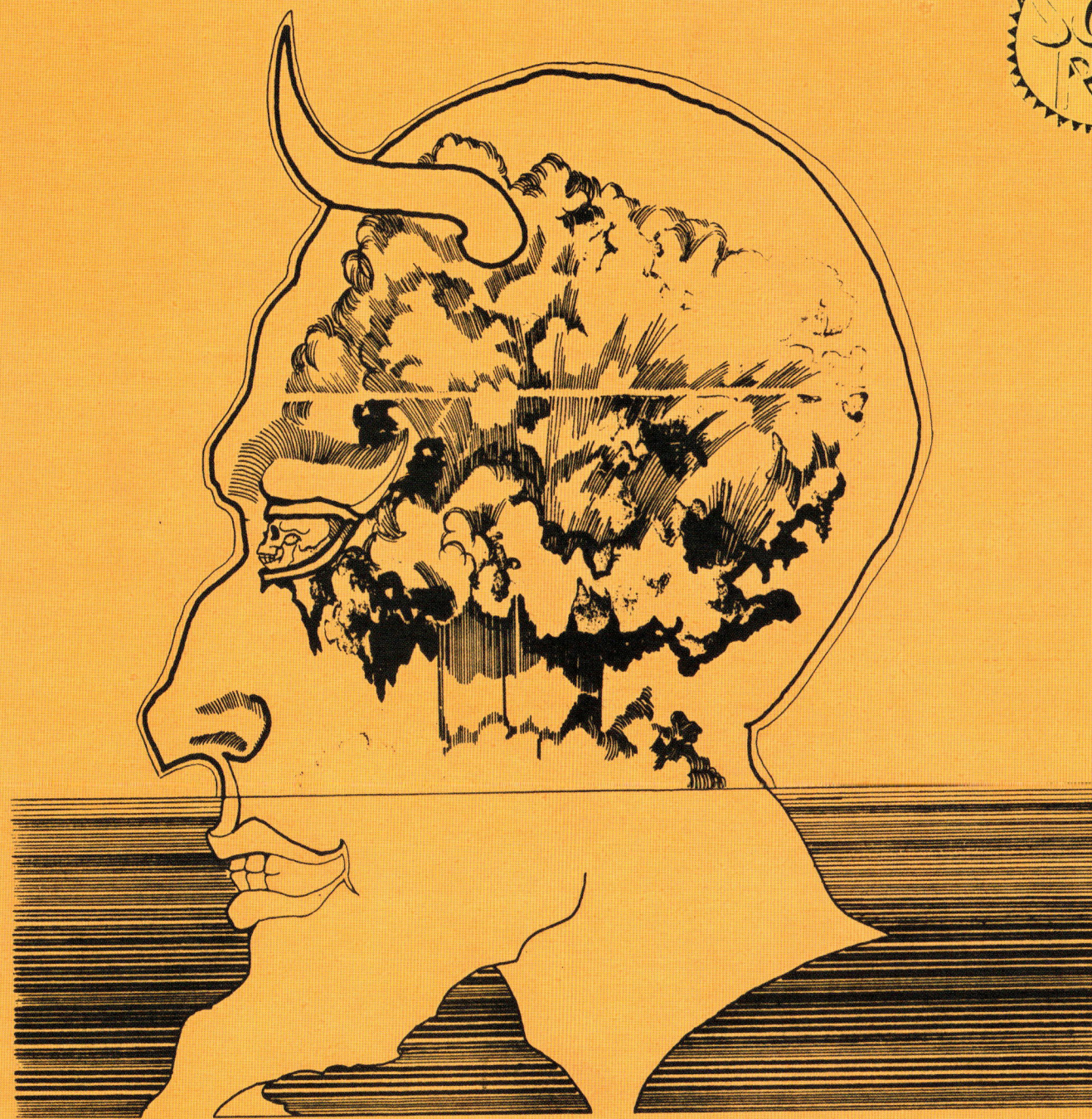

A FIRESIDE CHAT WITH LUCIFER

SUN RA
AND HIS ARKESTRA.

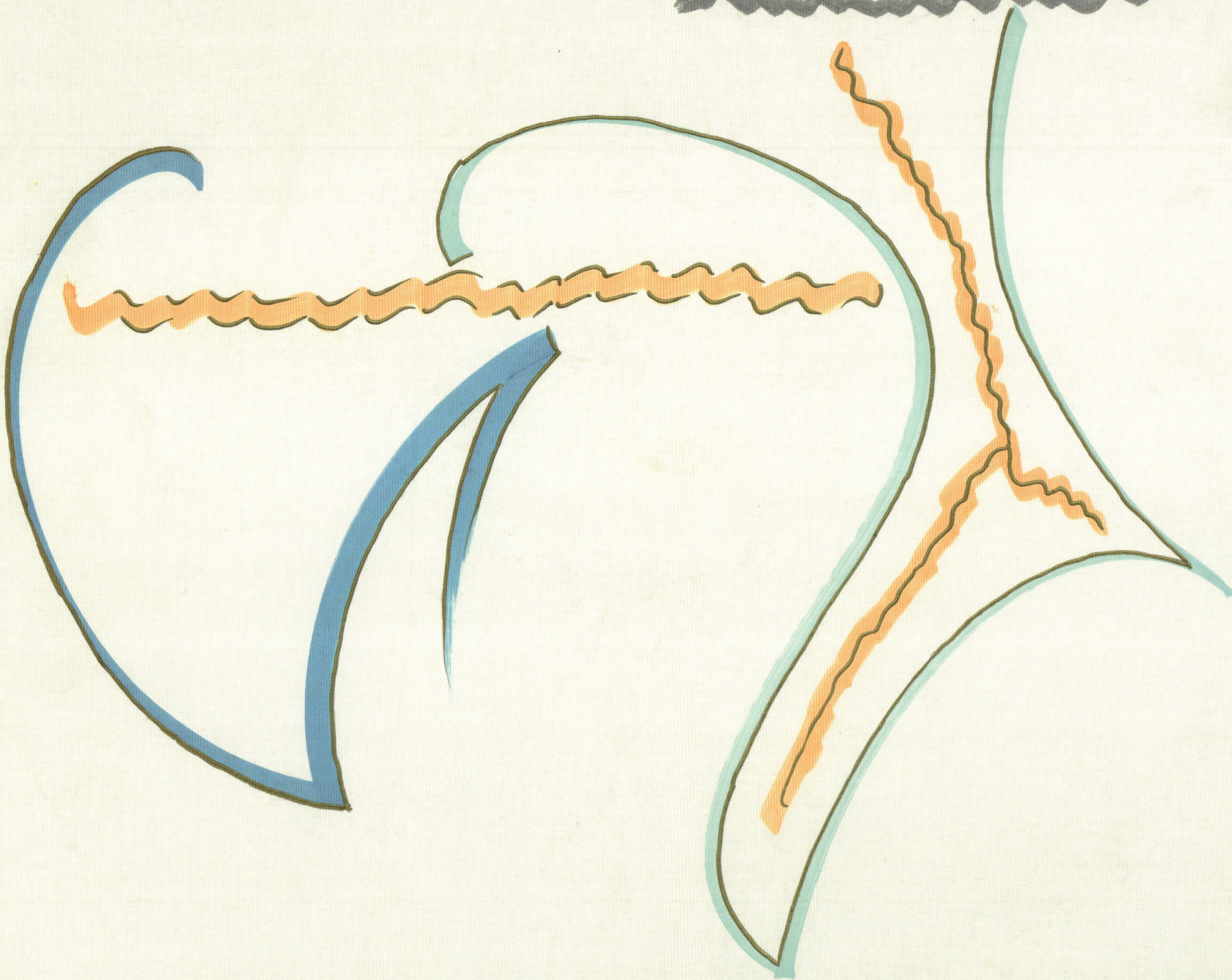

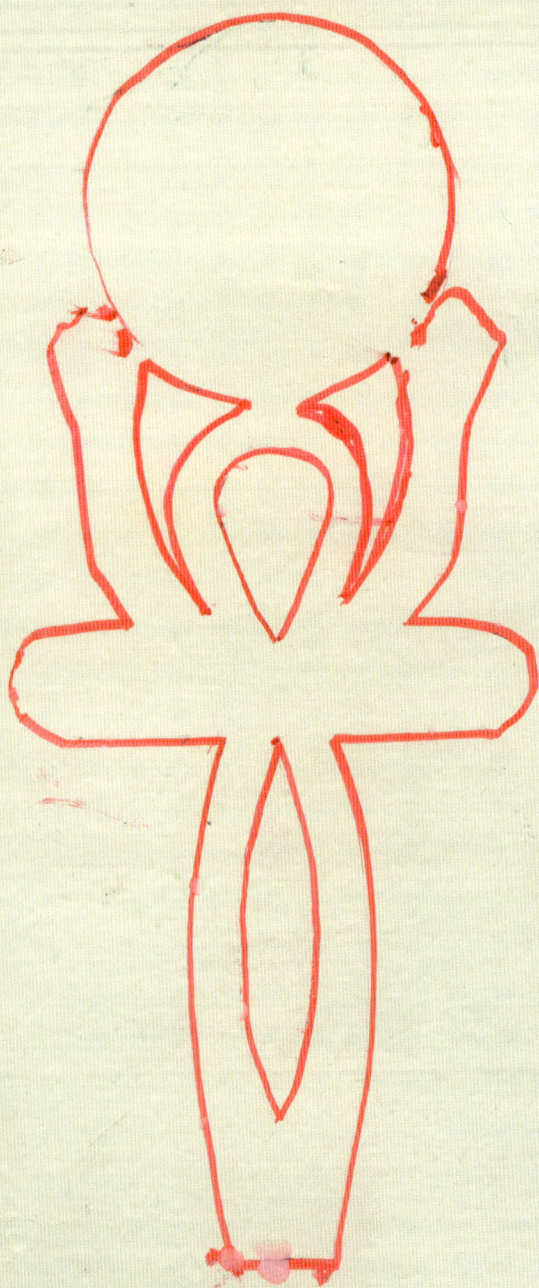

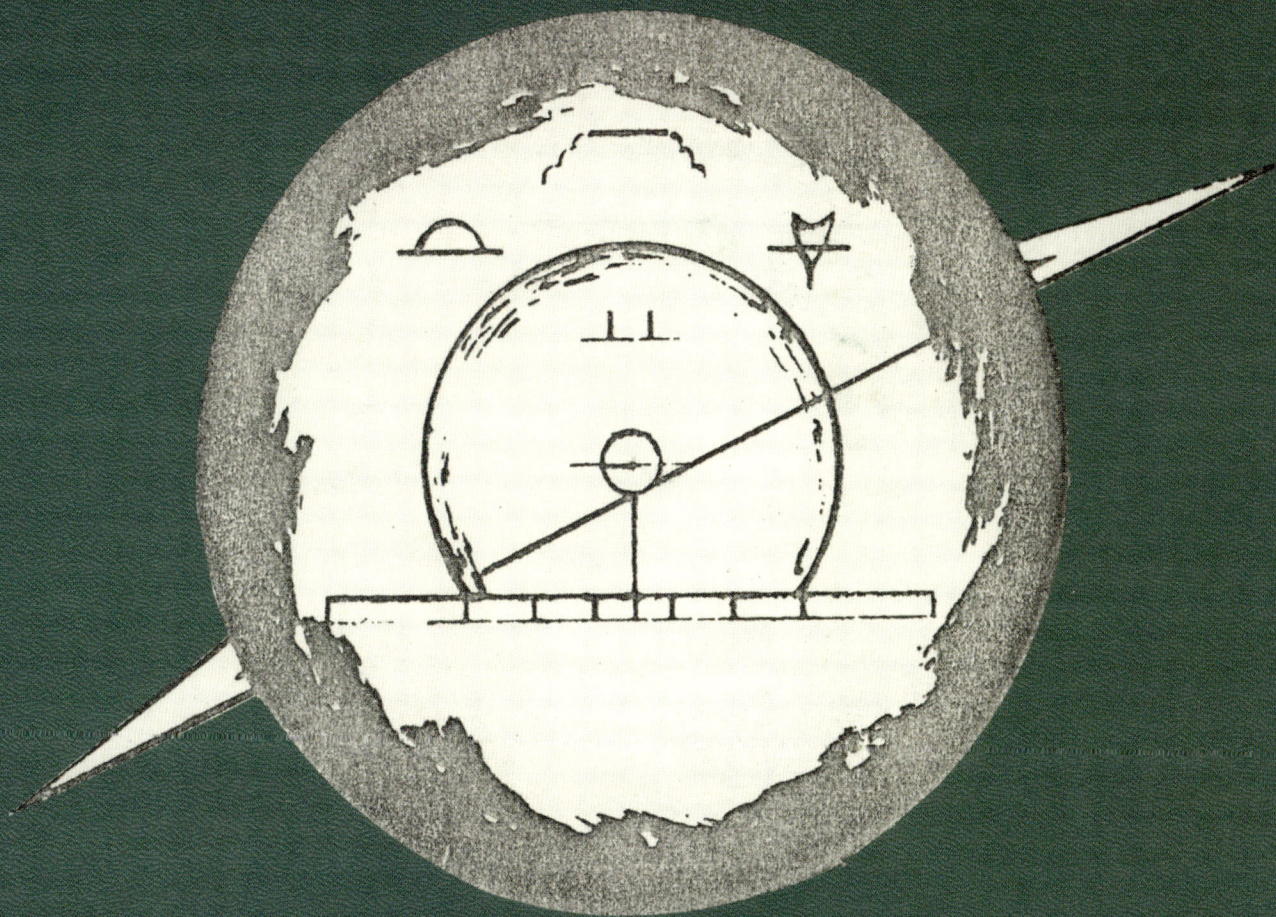

The Friends Of Skill

We must not say no to ourselves

When there is a greater deed to do

We must not say can't

If it is not imperative that we should

But we never should really believe that we can't

Whenever it is for our necessity good

We must not syncronize with anything less than art-wise dignity

It is either that we are natural-constructive-achievers

Or something less than the natural self.

The rendezvous time is here

I see a prophesy:

Across the thunder bridge of time

We rush with lightnin' feet

To join hands with those

THE FRIENDS OF SKILL

Who truly say and truly do.

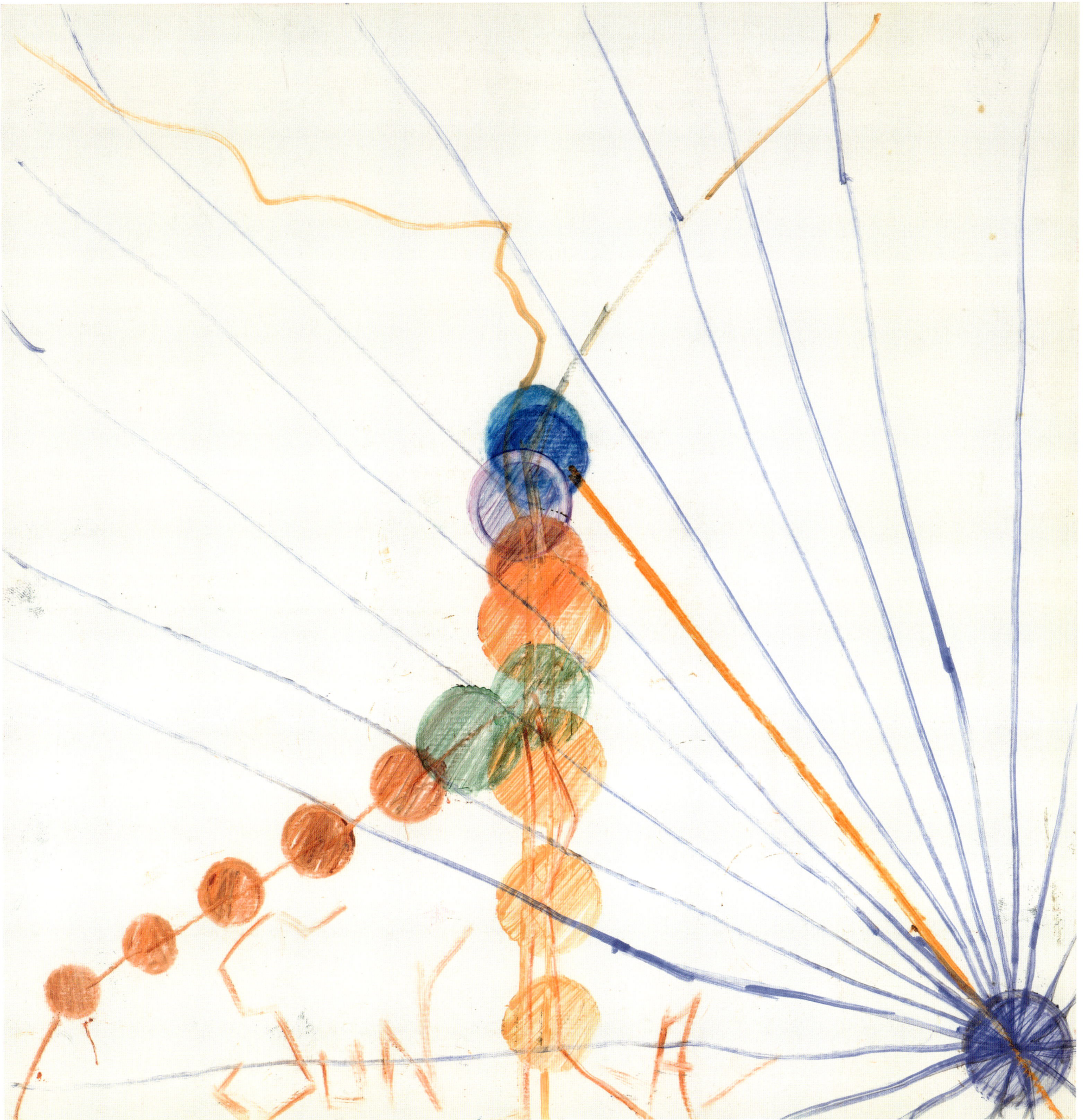

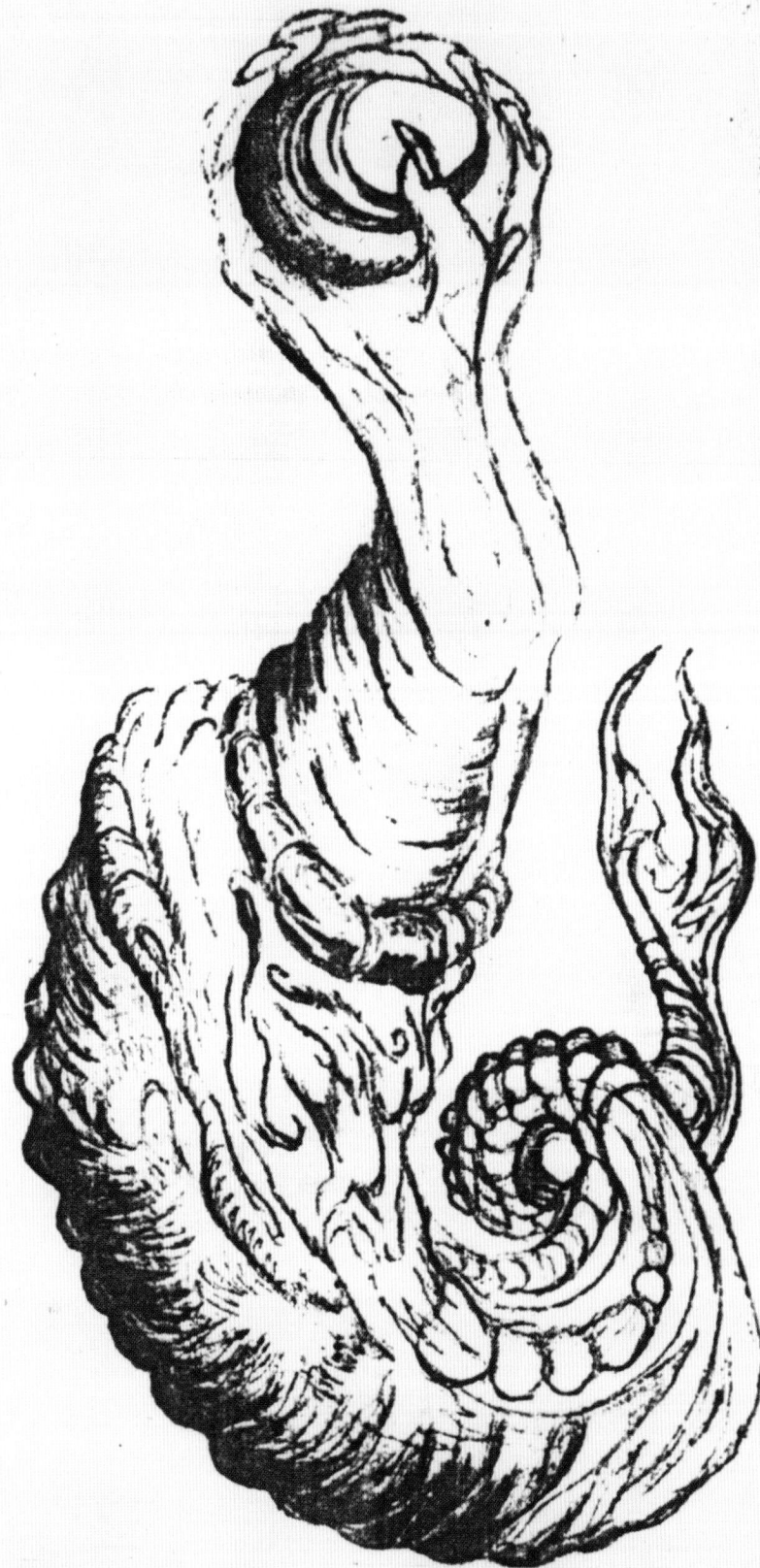

MEDIA DREAMS

1976

SUN RA SUN RA
10th MONTREUX FESTIVAL

SATURN RECORDS

SUN RA

MONTREUX VOL 1
1976

INTERPLANETARY CONCEPTS

145

SUN-RA MY BROTHER THE WIND

and his

ASTRO INFINITY

ARKESTRA

SUN-RA MY BROTHER THE WIND

and his

ASTRO
INFINITY
ARKESTRA

SUN RA MY BROTHER THE WIND

and his

ASTRO INFINITY ARKESTRA

SUN-RA MY BROTHER THE WIND

and his ASTRO INFINITY ARKESTRA

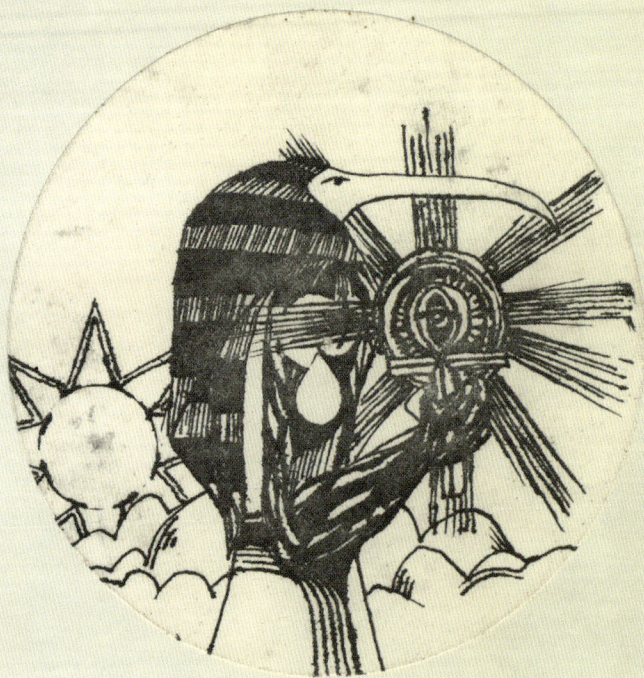

EGYPT

VOLUME I

SUN RA

NIGHT OF THE PURPLE MOON

$ 3 4 9

158

4/10/75

Nidhamu

Sun Ra & Astro-Intergalactic-Infinity-Arkestra
(Live in Egypt)
12/16/71

Side #1
Nidhamu

Side #2
Space Loneliness No. 2
Discipling No. 11
Discipling No. 15

El Saturn 77771

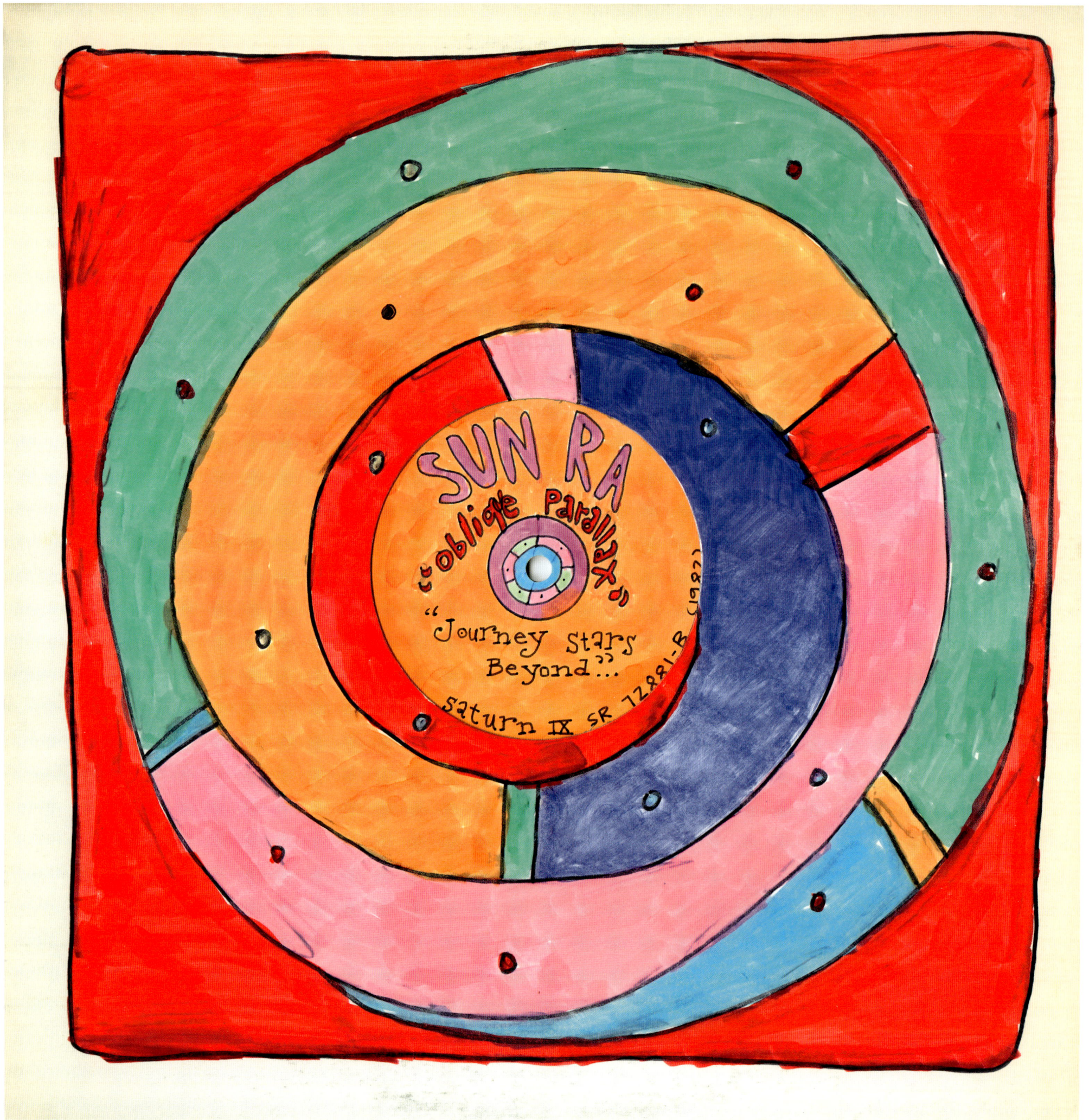

SUN RA
"oblique parallax"
"Journey Stars
Beyond..."
saturn IX SR 72881-B (1982)

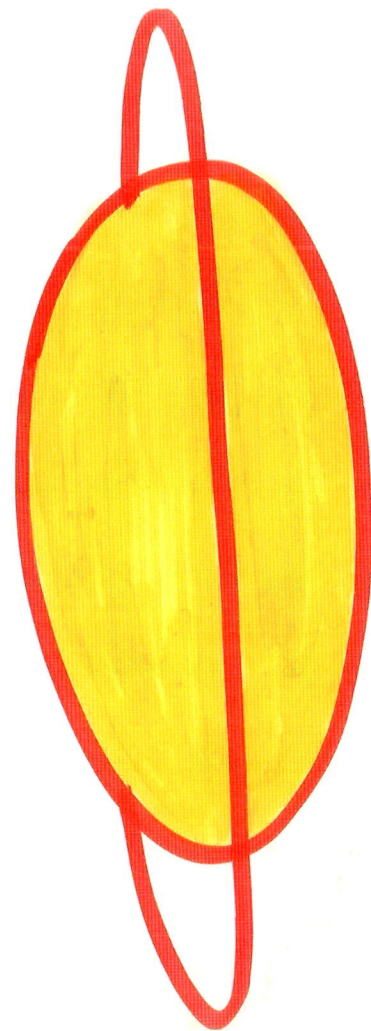

PARALLAX JOURNEY OBLIQUE

SUN RA

SUN RA

OMNIVERSE

VISITANT OF THE NINTH ULTIMATE

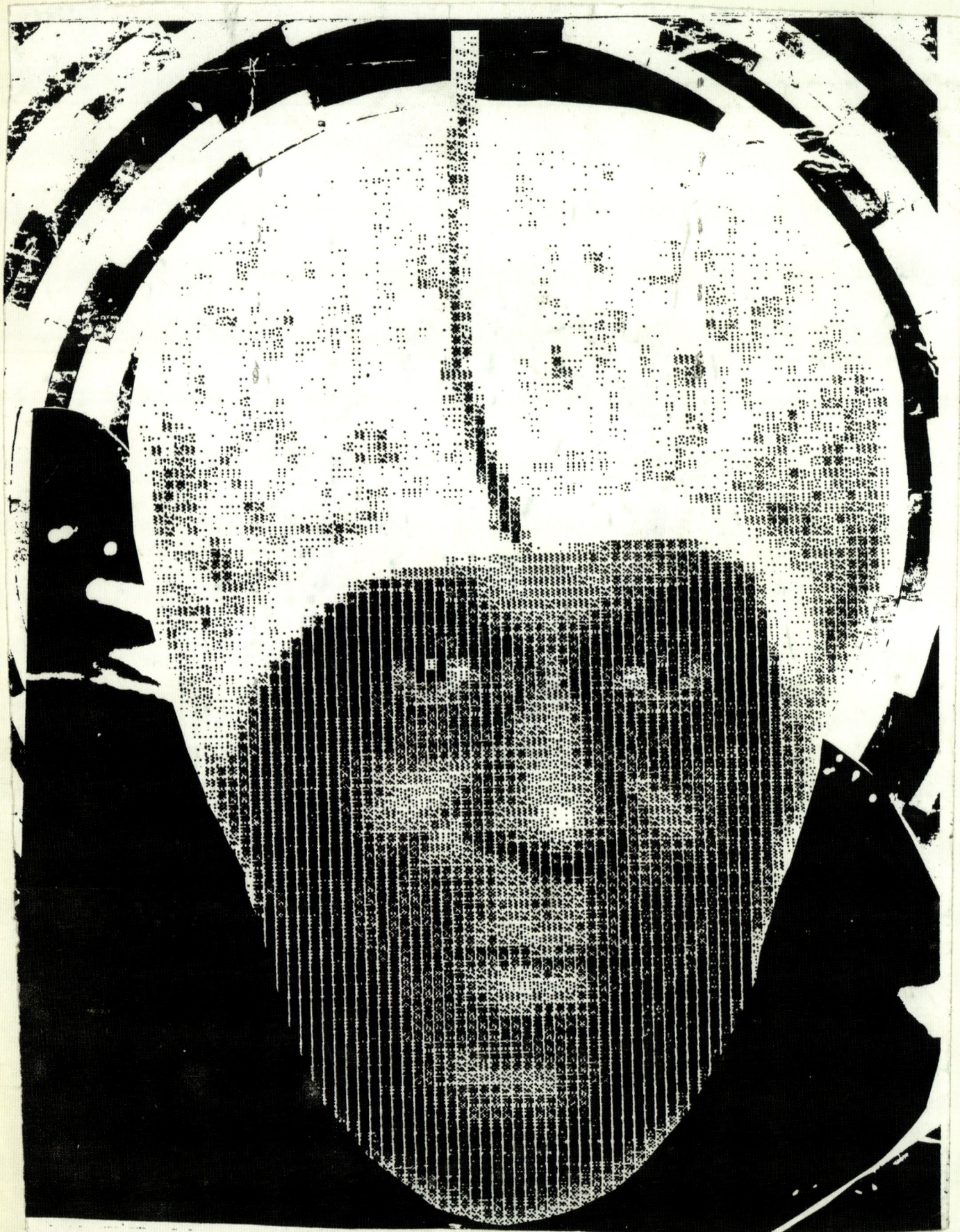

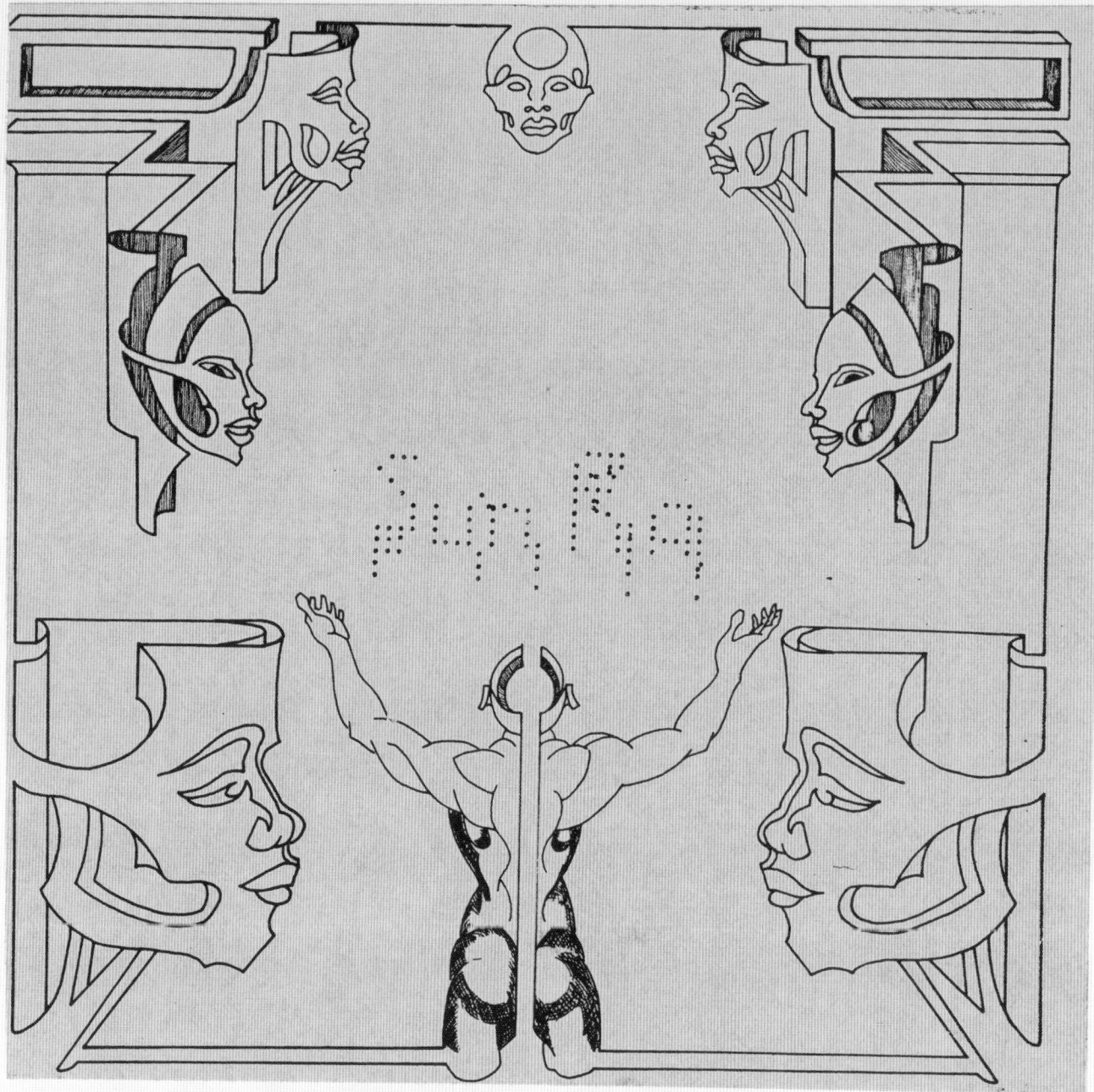

ON JUPITER

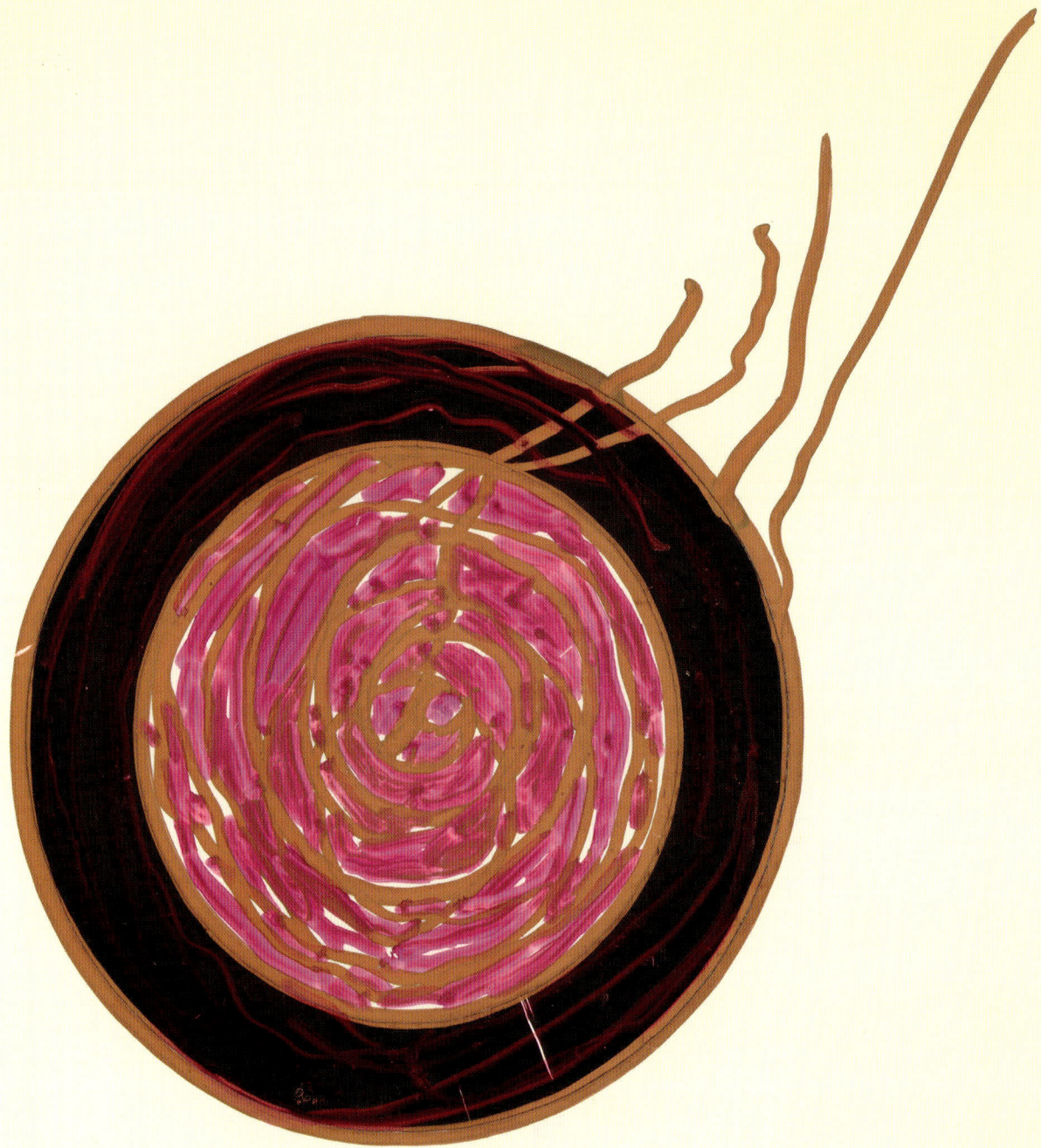

OVER THE RAINBOW

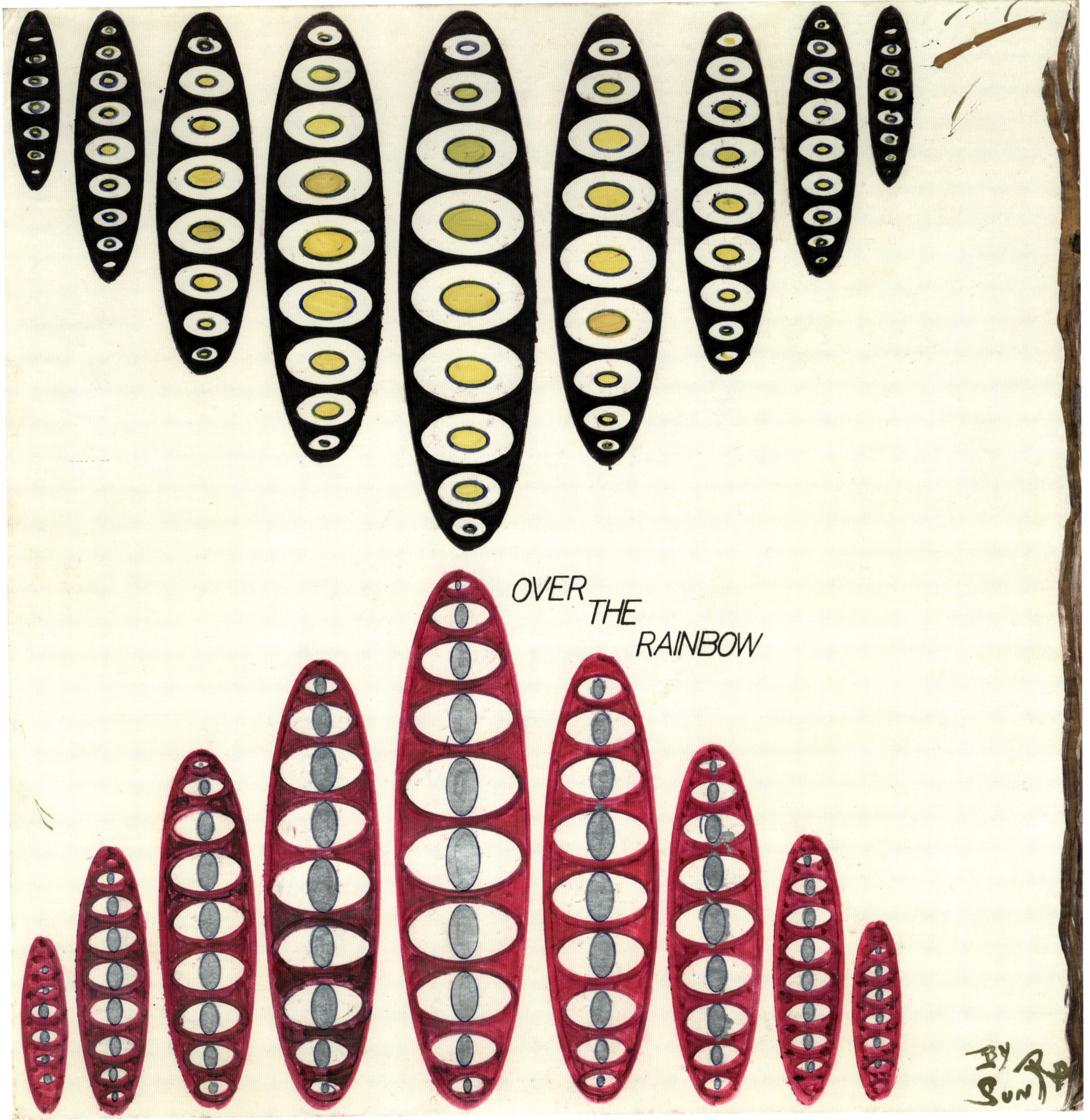

OVER THE RAINBOW

BY SUN RA

SUN RA & his Arkestra

DOOR OF THE COSMOS

SLEEPING BEAUTY

SLEEPING BEAUTY

SUN RA and HIS ARKESTRA

My Favorite Things

SUN-RA

INTERGALAXTIC RESEARCH
P. O. BOX 7124
CHICAGO, ILLINOIS, 60607

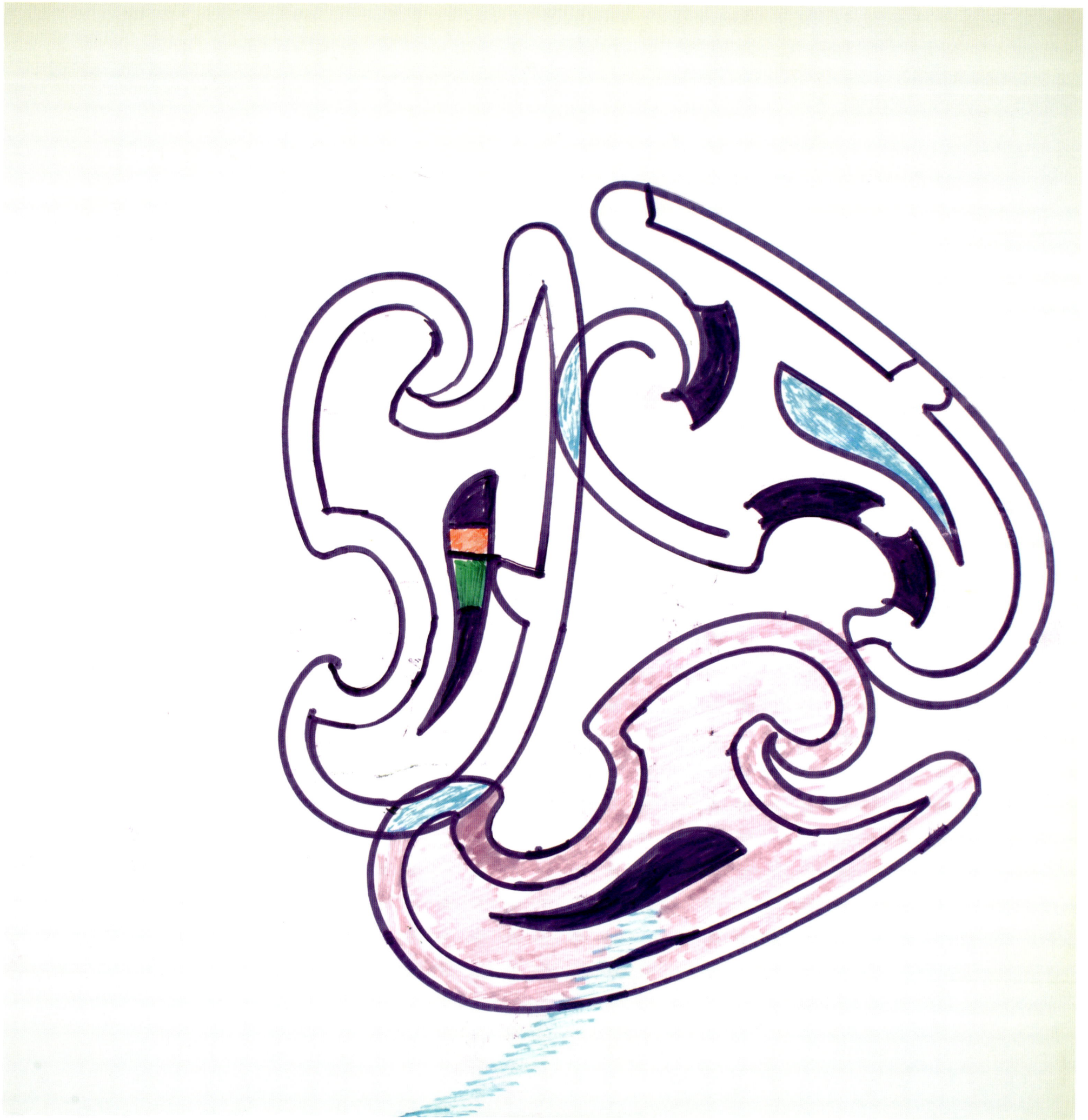

SATURN HANDMADE LABELS

SATURN

123180 A

enterplan bmi

© 1981 R

BEYOND THE PURPLE STAR ZONE
ROCKET NUMBER NINE
((Ra))

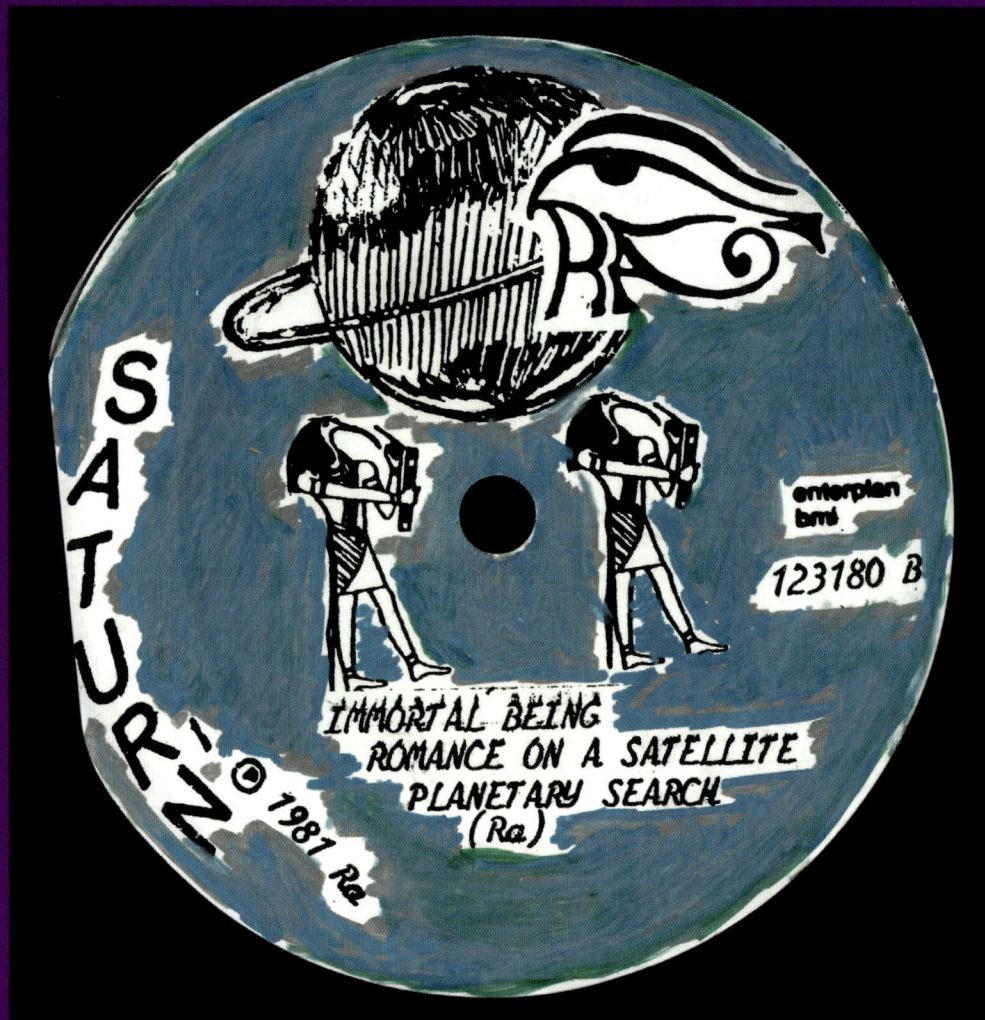

SATURN

enterplan bmi

123180 B

© 1981 Ra

IMMORTAL BEING
ROMANCE ON A SATELLITE
PLANETARY SEARCH
(Ra)

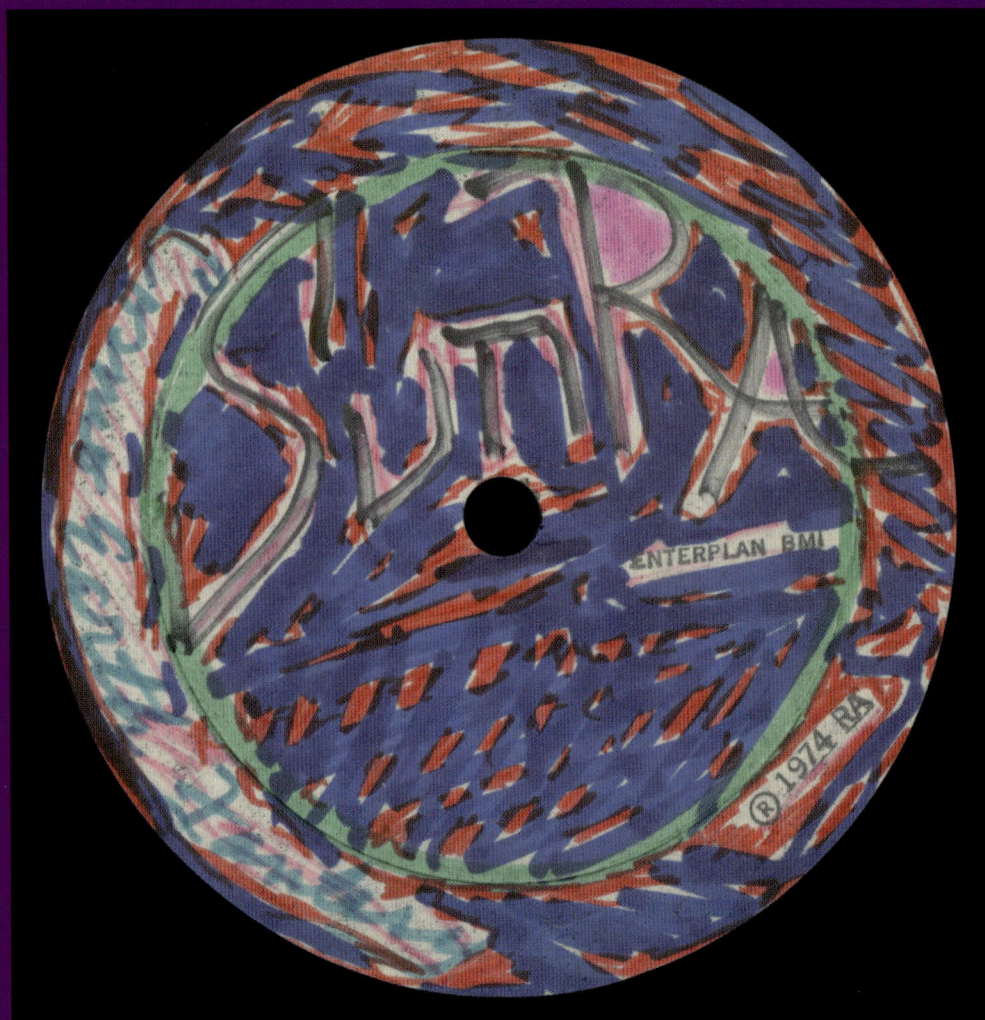

SUN RA

ENTERPLAN BMI

® 1974 RA

SUN RA

enterplan bmi

® 1974 RA

SIDE B,

Love Is For Always
The Song Of Drums
The World Of Africa

SUN RA

SIDE B.

Love Is For Alwa;

The Song Of Drums

The World Of Africa

enterplan

bmi

SUN RA

® 1974 RA

℗ 1977
SATURN

℗ 1977
SATURN

Love Is For Always
The Song Of Drums
The World Of Africa

SIDE B

SUN RA

© 1980
SATURN

enterplane
bmi

1981
A

INTENSITY
(Ra)
COSMO-ENERGY
(Ra)

© 1980
SATURN

enterplan
bmi

1981
B

DANCE OF INNOCENT PASSION

OMNISONICISM

compositions by
Sun Ra

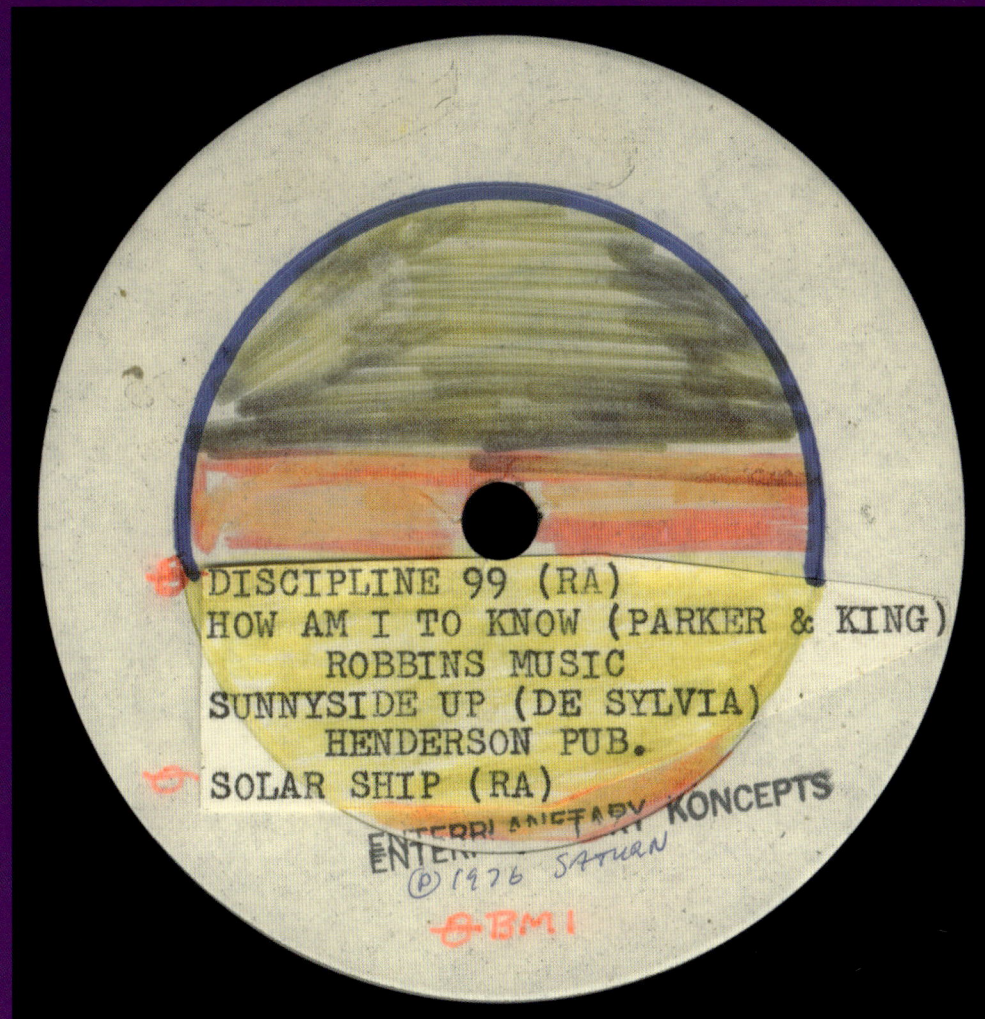

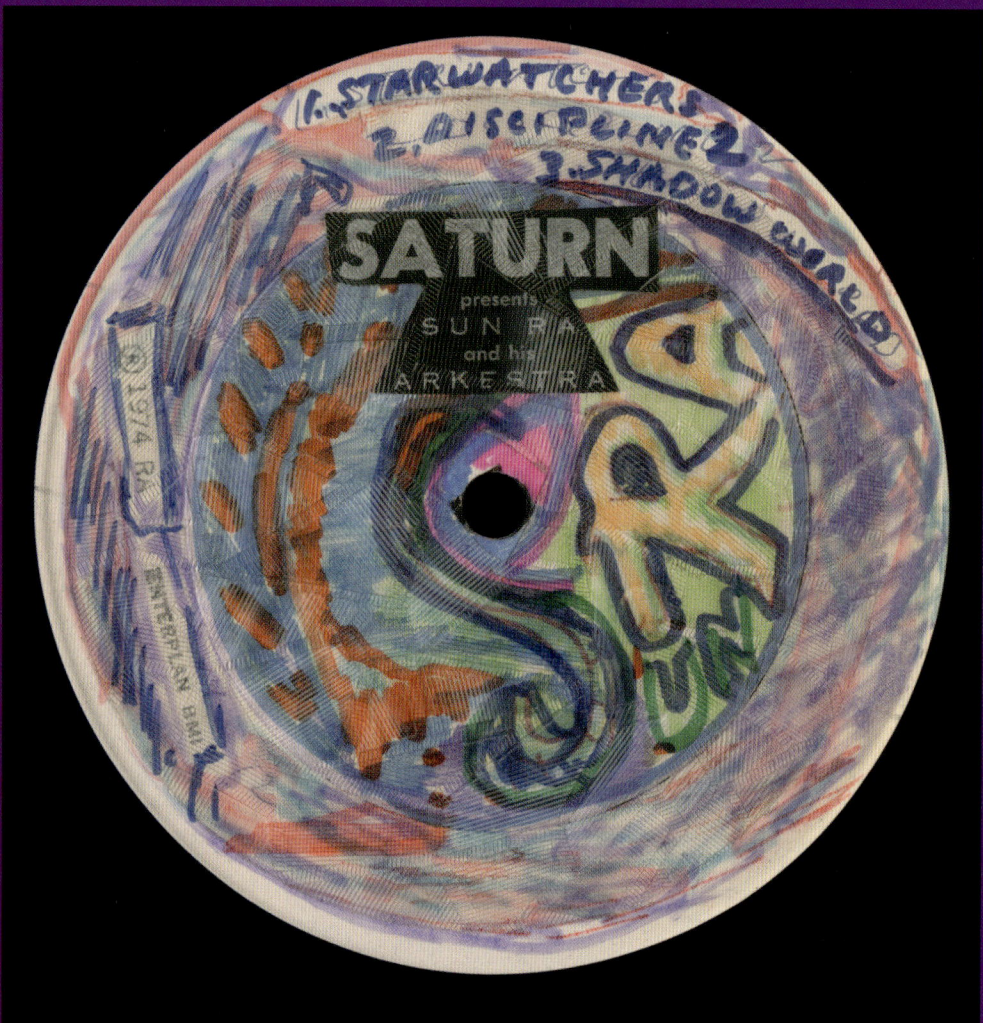

SUN RA AND HIS COSMO SWING ARKESTRA
EL SATURN
B
Enterplan Music BMI

EL
SATURN
presents
SUN RA and his ARKESTRA
SIDE
D
Montreux
(P)1976
SATURN
TAKE THE A TRAIN
(Strayhorn)

MONTREUX '76
MONTREUX '76
- CASCADES
- SOUND OF JOY
- PEOPLE
- WE TRAVEL THE SPACEWAYS

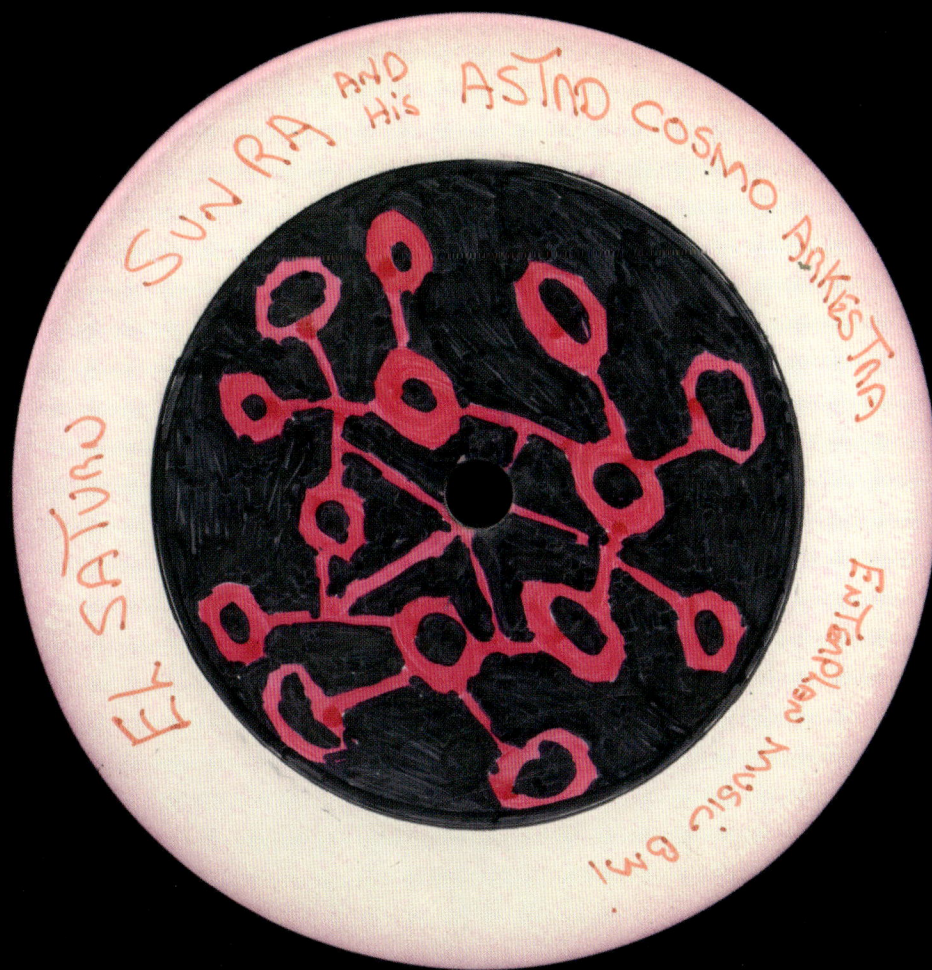

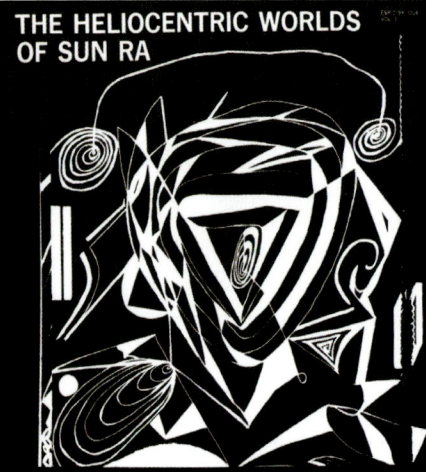

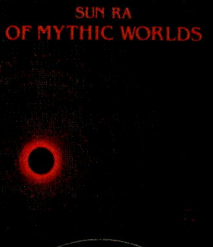

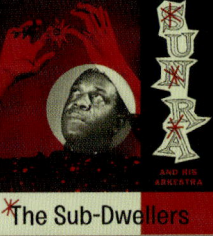

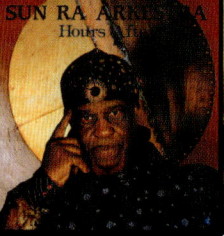

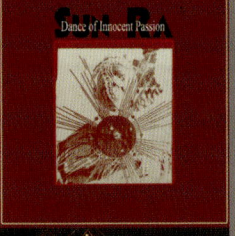

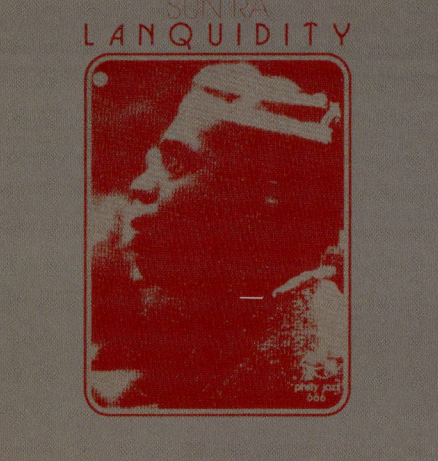

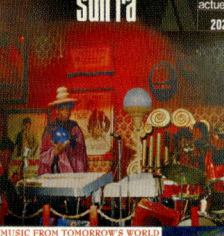

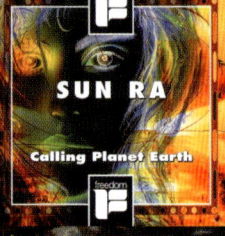

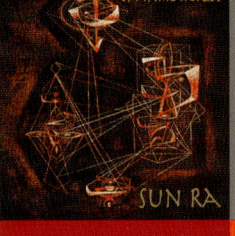

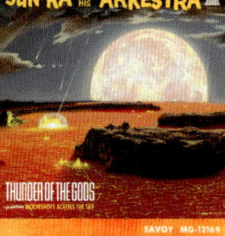

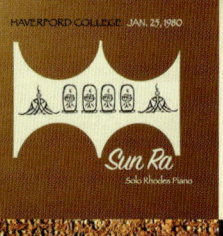

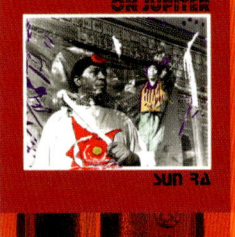

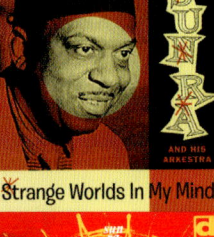

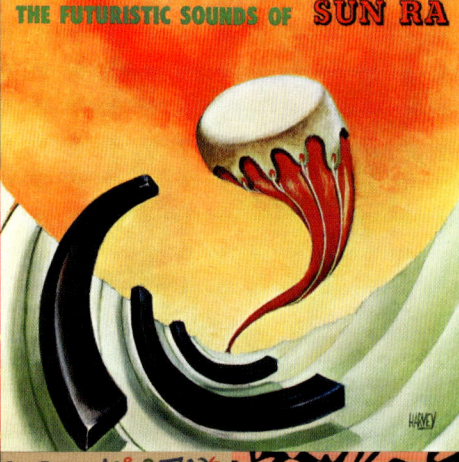

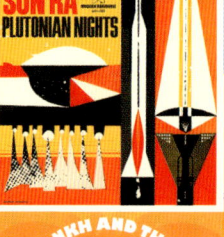

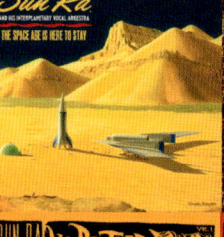

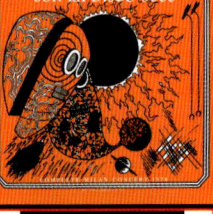

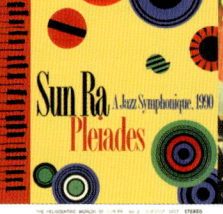

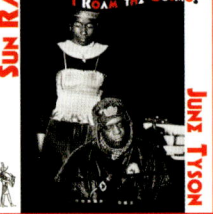

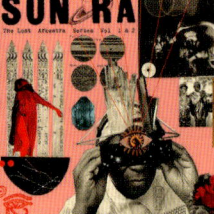

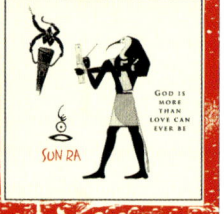

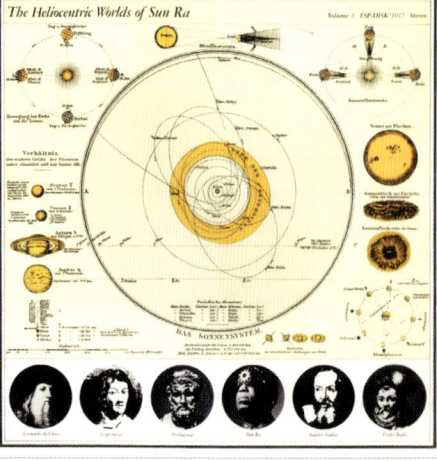

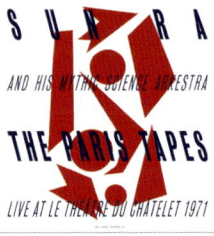

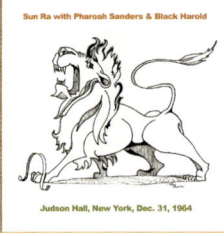

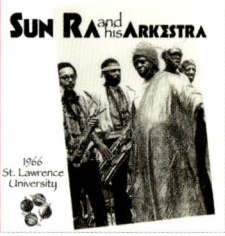